GIVING
IS NOT JUST
FOR THE VERY RICH

A HOW-TO GUIDE
FOR GIVING AND
PHILANTHROPY

GIVING
IS NOT JUST
FOR THE VERY RICH

A HOW-TO GUIDE
FOR GIVING AND
PHILANTHROPY

DR. SUSAN AURELIA GITELSON
foreword by ROBERT MORGENTHAU

RESPONSES TO <u>GIVING IS NOT JUST FOR THE VERY RICH</u>

"Gitelson successfully combines a discussion that raises important questions about an individual's attitudes toward giving with authoritative information about philanthropy in a volume that is nicely packaged and comprehensive in its scope. Her book lays the groundwork for the reader who has a sincere interest in making a contribution to a worthy cause."

ForeWord Clarion Reviews

"Straightforward prose, a handy table of contents, and worthwhile statistics and examples will help potential donors realize that no contribution is too small and that any amount of giving can bring happiness to the lives of all involved. The book is broken down into numerous categories, ranging from an examination of celebrities' charitable such as religious groups and higher education. The final section contains a helpful guide instructing readers how to identify reputable charities, how to choose organizations that are in alignment with one's own passions and how to ensure that donations are properly utilized… Readers with even a passing interest in charitable giving will find this guide to be an informative, go-to resource on how to get started."

"Gitelson (Multilateral Aid for National Development and Self-Reliance, 1975) draws upon her extensive background working with various international organizations to create an accessible, encyclopedic reference volume for average citizens interested in contributing to the greater good."

Kirkus Reviews

"I truly like the table of Contents. I think that you have covered the waterfront on subject matter and I think that the volume will be a valuable source for philanthropists and those interested in becoming one. I also think that charitable organizations will be interested in providing copies to prospects. The book will be a valuable resource."

Laurans A. Mendelson, Chairman of the Board, Chief Executive Officer and President, HEICO Aerospace Holdings Corp.

"Your book is timely and important. I am delighted to see the message that philanthropy is not just for the 1 percent! I admire what you have done with your own philanthropy. It is an inspiring example. I have always thought that the best gifts are those that are as meaningful for the giver as for the recipient. Good luck with the book! I hope it gets the wide audience that it deserves."

Dr. Joel H Rosenthal, President, Carnegie Council for Ethics in International Affairs

"A must read for all who strive to creatively promote the betterment of humanity."

Dr. George D. Schwab, President, National Committee on American Foreign Policy

"Having worked with many philanthropic clients, I share Dr. Gitelson's point of view regarding the multi-faceted values of giving." Giving Is Not Just for the Very Rich" shows the giver how to optimize philanthropy and provides an indispensable primer on why-to-do-it and how-to-do-it."

Arlene G. Dubin, family law attorney at Moses & Singer LLP in New York and author of "Prenups for Lovers: A Romantic Guide to Prenuptial Agreements"

"Giving Is Not Just For The Very Rich: A How To Guide For Giving and Philanthropy" is clearly a MUST-READ book for those who want to address the needs of students, teachers, supervisors and parents. As the educator and researcher, Ron Edmonds said many years ago, "We can make a real difference, it depends upon how much we CARE". The examples cited in this book clearly reflect actions taken by those who CAR. It will also provide Best practices guidance to everyone who has the human and financial capital to make That difference because they also CARE for all to have HIGH EXPECTATION.

Dr. Charlotte K. Frank, Sr. Vice President-Research & Development, McGraw-Hill Education

"I very much liked the clarity and directness of the writing. It clearly, as indicated by the chapter on how to evaluate charities, would be a useful book for many people. I can also see it as a book that people give as a present to others at birthdays and holidays."

Dr. Michael Curtis Distinguished Professor Emeritus of Political Science, Rutgers University

"Dr. Susan Gitelson has created an ambitious compendium of examples of philanthropy from names familiar to us all like Wendy Kopp, Mark Zuckerberg and Bill Gates to those unknown to most. All donors share the desire to improve life and create equality of education opportunity for all. How the reader can do it is what Gitelson explains in clear and precise prose."

"This book is compelling reading for young and old and illuminates the path to helping others while enriching one's own life."

Dr. Pola Rosen, Publisher, Education Update

"Dr. Gitelson, like community foundations, believes everyone has a role to play in helping build community, making the places they love even better now and for generations to come."

**Fraser Nelson, Executive Director,
Community Foundation of Utah**

Table of Contents

Dedication

To my parents, Dr. Moses Leo and Miriam Gitelson,
In gratitude for their inspiration

Foreword

by Robert M. Morgenthau

I can date my own decision to dedicate my life to giving back to April 20,1944, when I was in the chilly waters of the Mediterranean having survived the sinking of my ship, the *Lansdale*, with the loss of 44 officers and men. Although I did not have much bargaining power, I made a deal with the almighty that if I made it out alive, I would dedicate my life to the public good. It was no surprise, I supposed, that I chose this direction. After all, I had in my father and grandfather two paradigms for the principle that we all have an important responsibility to give back. Through a combination of public service and philanthropy, these two men provided me with inspiring examples of underscored for me what Winston Churchill is said to have said about philanthropy: "You make a living by what you get; you make a life by what you give."

In my long career of public service, I have dedicated myself to two causes in particular – the *Police Athletic League* (PAL) and the *Museum of Jewish Heritage – A Living Memorial to the Holocaust*. I have been privileged to serve these two great institutions as chairman for many years, and, along the way, I have helped to raise a great deal of money from a wide variety of people at every level of giving. One thing can be said of all of them – they were made better by what they gave. Their involvement in helping others invariably helped them. And I count my own contributions – in time and effort as well as in dollars and cents – as among the most meaningful that I can imagine.

Dr. Susan Gitelson has chosen an important topic for this book, and a key part of her message is in the title, itself-- *Giving Is Not Just For The Very Rich*. Giving is for all of us, who, in our own ways, have the power and the capacity to make a difference. By giving we affirm not just our own values, but we make a statement to others. We receive something that we cannot buy but can only get by giving.

Robert M. Morgenthau
Wachtell, Lipton, Rosen & Katz

I.

INTRODUCTION
GIVING BENEFITS OTHERS
AND YOURSELF

Do you want to help others with your abilities, ideas, and assets?
Then you will wish to decide what your major values and
motivations are and how you can do something worthwhile. As
you examine yourself and analyze how you can be most effective in
giving to others, you are likely to enhance your own life. Concern
for others often leads simultaneously to greater joy for yourself.

We will help you better understand how to give to others effectively by first offering many examples of what other people are doing to give you ideas of where you may want to put your efforts. Second, we will delineate major areas of giving and provide leads for you to pursue further. Third, we will offer information on evaluating different charities to decide how effective they are. Finally, we will suggest ways to deal with your possible choices and commitments so that your contributions can have the greatest impact.

GIVING BACK

Are you fortunate enough in good or difficult economic times to be in a position where you can give back to others to help them advance through education and training? Or have you recovered from an illness and want to support research about the causes and alleviate suffering for others? Have you been collecting artwork or other precious objects and now you want to share them with a larger audience? As you think through what you want to do and with whom, you will gain many insights into your own values and priorities. What are your real purposes in life? How can you express them best through giving of yourself and your assets? Which institutions and organizations are most significant to you? How can you feel confident that the leaders of a particular institution are likely to carry out purposes they say they will? Should you give to many worthwhile causes or concentrate on only one?

It is never too early and never too late to start giving back! Some people begin when they are very young and want to share a part of their allowance or their first earned money with people who have less. Others feel they have to concentrate on getting through school, launching their careers, families, etc., and only later feel they are finally in a position to contribute to charity. Some choose their cause or causes because of their lifetime values and affiliations. Others respond to a particular situation, such as a natural disaster or illness or malnutrition in the US or abroad.

There are so many worthwhile causes and the giving process enriches life for both donors and recipient so much that whenever you are ready, there will be plenty for you to undertake. We will give you a wide variety of ideas about what to do and how to maximize your contributions to accomplish more for others while enhancing your own life.

While we will offer example from wealthiest donors, we will also indicate how much is being done by people who are not very rich. The common thread is to show people who are improving the world in varied ways that benefit others and simultaneously enhance their own lives. Bear in mind that the value of your activities does not depend only on your giving money. You can accomplish a great deal as a government official or a nonprofit professional. You can also spearhead programs through your favorite organizations or place of worship or through social media.

WHY ALTRUISM CAN GIVE YOU PLEASURE

People who give are usually happier than those who do not, according to the Social Capital Community Benchmark Survey of thirty thousand American households in 2000. They found that 43 percent of those who gave money to charity were more likely than non-givers to indicate they were "very happy." Among volunteers, 42 percent were more content than non-volunteers. Basically, those who gave money or time to religious or secular causes were happier than non-givers. Similarly, those who give are less likely to be unhappy or depressed, according to the University of Michigan's Panel Study of income Dynamic in 2001. Helping others releases brain chemicals called endorphins, which reduce stress and can cause euphoria, which some psychologists call "helper's high."[1] The American Psychological Association has reported that people who give emotional and material support to relatives, friends, and neighbors are more likely to live longer.[2] Moreover, Nicholas D. Kristof, based on David J. Linden's *The Compass of Pleasure*, reports that "generosity… often exhilarates us." About half of the people in one study reported more pleasure from giving money that from receiving it. The basic finding is that "altruism and generosity can be hedonistic pleasures."[3]

MAJOR FEATURES OF AMERICA PHILANTHROPY

Americans have been extremely generous even in difficult times, giving around $300 billion a year to charitable causes. Compared to other countries as a percentage of gross domestic product (GDP), the US has been first, with around 2 percent annually. Britain has been giving around 0.73 percent, and France 0.14 percent. Other countries have been giving less, but a major reason outside the US is that the state supports most institutions, so they do not have to depend as much on private contributions.[4]

Although the amounts Americans have been giving have changed over time, especially as a result of economic difficulties, the percentage by categories has remained quite steady. Generally, about one-third goes to religion, which includes education, social welfare, and many other activities organized along denominational lines. Education has been second, with about 13 percent, including gifts to schools pre-kindergarten through high school (P-12), collages, universities, and libraries. The third-highest category comes from gifts to grant-making private, community, and operating foundations, with about 10 percent. Next come human services organizations, including responses to natural disasters, like earthquakes and hurricanes, and economic crises, with emergency care and supplies. Many people give through public-society benefit organizations and umbrella funds, such as United Ways, Jewish federations, and donor-advised funds. Hospitals, cancer care, and other health organizations make up the next category. Following them are international affairs (including development, aid and relief) organizations to protect the environment and animals.[5] While the wealthiest donor often get the most attention, about 65 percent of households with less than

$100,000 gave to charity in 2006.[6] One study showed that working-age Americans making $50,000 to $100,000 a year give a higher percentage, even two to six times more, of their whole income to charity than do those making more than $10 million.[7]

Generally, individual giving came to 75 percent of total 2009 giving. Combined individual bequest, and estimated family foundation donations reached 88 percent of the 2009 total. The rest was contributed by foundations and corporations.[8]

Women have been increasing their role in philanthropy. They often are the main decision-makers in many families for where contribution should go. Those women who have their own incomes give more than men with similar incomes.[9]

Since there were 1.2 million or more charitable foundations in the US in 2009, up from around eight hundred thousand in 2000,[10] it is important to be very selective and careful in making contributions.

SOURCES FOR THIS BOOK

Many vivid examples of giving have come from reading *The Chronicle of Philanthropy, The New York Times, the Wall Street Journal* (particularly "The Donor of the Day" column), Forbes, Fortune, and other publications, as well as the websites of many charities and rating agencies. I have also gained many insights through personal encounters with both leading philanthropists and givers from a wide range of backgrounds who may give more ideas and time than money. It has been an ongoing pleasure to research so many exemplary people and causes, while at the same time trying to evaluate their effectiveness and noting negative features where they occur.

In addition, I have benefitted from reading books about philanthropy and giving by **President Bill Clinton, Charles Bronfman and Jeffrey Solomon, Thomas J. Tierney and Joel L. Fleishman,** and others (see selected bibliography).

MY LIFELONG ASSOCIATION WITH GIVING
HAS LED ME TO WRITE THIS BOOK

I have been involved with philanthropy since I was a child because my father, **Dr. Moses Leo Gitelson,** a businessman "with a Ph.D. on the side," was devoted to giving book collections and microfilms of rare books and manuscripts to major universities and other educational institutions, such as **Columbia University** and the **New York Public Library.** He once told me when I was very young that we had two valuable books printed before 1500. Should we keep them for ourselves, he asked me, or should we give them to a friend of his, the librarian of an institution of higher learning, who wanted them to attain the library's accreditation in New York State? I replied immediately that we should give them to the library. This tradition has led me to give my rare book collection to the **New York University (NYU)** rare books library and a variety of collections to Columbia University, the **Hebrew University of Jerusalem,** and other institutions. Sometimes when I ask the institutions staff members, "Don't you have many other donors sharing their treasures with you?" I am often surprised that the answer is, "Very few." That is why I have become such a strong advocate of philanthropy, with the slogan: "the more you give to others the happier you are likely to become."

My father also established several awards in memory of his father, **Nehemiah Gitelson,** just after he died in 1932, beginning with a medal for "The Spirit of the Search for Truth" at my father's alma mater, **City College of New York.** He also founded an award for Jewish communal leadership at his fraternity, **Alpha Epsilon Pi,** at both the undergraduate and alumni levels. He began with the AEPi Alpha Chapter at New York University, where he had received his M.B.A. and Ph.D. This award is still being given and has inspired many medalists to go on to major contributions in communal leadership, according to **Philip H. Cohen,** a medalist, who subsequently established his own communal leadership award at the fraternity modeled on my father's awards.

From the time I was nine years old, my father had me help him with his award presentations. He also encouraged me from the age of ten to attend board meetings where he was a member and to speak publicly to adult audiences. (My mother loved the arts but was not proactive like my father. Since my father did not have any sons and my older sister was not very interested in public speaking, he turned to me to share his ideas and projects, which transformed my life.)

Subsequently, when I started to give awards and various book and other collections to universities, I did almost everything in my father's memory. More recently, since I do not have any children, I have used my own name more frequently. Please see the higher education and awards chapters for a fuller description of the programs I have been sponsoring for more than thirty years.

My core idea and the title appeared in an article I wrote "Giving Is Not Just for the Very Rich," e-published in **Good News**, December 1, 2005, in which I started:

Have you ever read about multi-million-dollar contributions from Bill Gates or another mogul and felt, (How does this apply to me? I could never do anything on that scale!"

That may be true, but do you realize how much you can do to help other people?

If you are a loving parent or grandparent, and at the same time contributing to a better community. Teachers, librarians, social workers, humane doctors, human rights advocates, and so many dedicated people are contributing mightily to improve our civil society. Those who give to others are generally much happier than those people, such as the "Desperate Housewives," who are often bored and dissatisfied and don't realize the joys that come from nurturing others!

HOW TO USE THIS BOOK TO ENCOURAGE YOUR PASSIONS AND CARRY THEM OUT EFFECTIVELY

Since you have decided you want to give to others with maximum impact, this book will help you examine your values and motivations, decide which institutions can best carry out your goals, and become an active, creative, and innovative giver.

How can you narrow down what you want to be your special contribution?

To do so, what are your deepest concerns and purposes?

Which institution(s) should you choose in a particular category. e.g., school, hospital, museum. etc.? What programs do they offer? Which constituencies do they serve? How effective are they?

For example. Transparency: what percentage of the funds they collect actually go to the cause and how much to overhead?

Are they pioneers, innovators or leaders in their fields, or are they duplicating and overlapping with other similar organizations?

If they did not exist. Would they really be missed?

Who are the leaders? Do you know them personally? Have you been impressed favorably by what you have read about them?

This book will help you zero in on the areas and organizations that interest you the most. It will also provide guidelines for checking out the qualifications of various charities. There will be examples of how some people have launched special programs that might inspire you.

Remember from the outset, while it would be desirable to be able to give millions of dollars to the institutions of your choice, you can make valuable contributions for much less money if you devise effective program. In addition, you can provide invaluable assistance by conceptualizing and implementing special projects to help less advantaged students, people suffering from particular diseases, etc. In truth, your time and energies alone can be very valuable for improving the world.

As people who are already giving to others in special ways can tell you, your life will be enriched greatly when you volunteer to implement existing programs and causes you believe in, or when you devise special programs to help others and then carry them out. The process of empathizing with others can help alleviate your preoccupation with your own problems. The interaction with people who need you enhances your sense of wellbeing. When you ask yourself, "What am I doing that is worthwhile?" you can reassure yourself that you have created and supported programs and projects that are benefiting others.

My goal is to guide you to find meaning and pleasure in helping others in myriad ways. I will give a significant portion of the proceeds from this book to charity since one of the greatest joys of having money, ideas, and energy is to share them with others.

II.

DIFFERENT KINDS OF IMPASSIONED GIVING FOR MAXIMUM EFFECT

A. WEALTHIEST DONORS WHO ARE PACESETTERS

America has produced many billionaires in the past decades – most of them self-made entrepreneurs and investors. As with rich people through the ages and around the world, the first thought for many may be a lavish lifestyle. The media delight in showing the newly minted rich, as well as those with inherited wealth, with many homes, cars, private jets, and possibly a huge yacht. At the same time, many of the wealthiest individuals are concerned with giving back to society and are searching for ways to do this most effectively. As **Eli Broad** has said, "Philanthropy is hard work. Many people think it's easy to give money away. We want our wealth to make a measurable impact." Broad is one of the twelve Americans out of eighteen self-made billionaires worldwide who have given at least $1 billion to charity.[1]

The wealthiest donors are important both for their actual contributions and for the examples they set for other people. The individuals we will cite here are significant also because they have taken a hands-on approach to their giving, which can be emulated at any level. Foremost among them is **Bill Gates**, who was estimated by *Forbes* in 2010 to be worth $56 billion and to have given $28 billion through the **Bill and Melinda Gates Foundation**, making it the largest in the US and the world. With the motto "All Lives Have Equal Development, including agriculture, financial services, water, sanitation and hygiene, reducing poverty, and increasing opportunities; Global Health, which focuses on fighting and preventing HIV/AIDS, malaria, tuberculosis, and other diseases; and the United States, with priorities on education, libraries, the Pacific Northwest, and related areas (www.gatesfouncation.org). With their help, a vaccine has been developed by Glaxo to protect children against malaria.[2]

Bill Gates emphasizes his desire to learn and to benefit from experience. He says the "key is picking things that if they work have huge impact. So inventing a vaccine is that way. Helping to rethink how education could be done using the internet is that way… And, amazingly, there tends to be an underinvestment in these areas."[3]

Melinda Gates searches for "strategic intervention points" based on the "belief that every human being has equal worth," which leads to action to bring greater equity in health and education and other fields.[4] in October 2011, she hosted a conference on "behavior change" for top social scientists and major health advocates to discuss how to ensure that people actually use the technologies the foundation is delivering.[5]

The second-wealthiest American, **Warren Buffett,** who was said to have $50 billion in 2010, had given $8.3 billion, mainly through the Gates Foundation.[6] For the most of his life, he had not thought much about philanthropy, but in 2006 he decided to give a large part of his Berkshire Hathaway fortune, approximately $30 billion, to the Bill and Melinda Gates Foundation. He also gave money to some other Buffett family foundation, including $1 billion to the funds of each of his three children.[7]

Gates and Buffett have set out to persuade other billionaires and very wealthy people to give more than half of their wealth to charity during their lifetime or at death in the **"Giving Pledge"** announced in 2010. By the following year, around seventy billionaires had signed up. One of them, **Lynn Schusterman,** said she wanted "to continue working to encourage others, including emerging philanthropists of all ages and all capacities, to join us in seeking to repair the world: the further we broaden our reach, the more we will benefit from a diversity of people, perspectives and approaches as we strive to tackle problems of common concern" (www.givingpledge.org).

Among the other American donors cited by Forbes who have already given more than $1 billion are **George Soros, Eli Broad, Michael Bloomberg, Ted Turner,** and **Jon Huntsman, Sr.** within our limited space, we will expand a bit on them and on other innovative donors. as appropriate we will also examine other significant givers, such as **Chuck Feeney, Pierre Omidyar, Jeff Skoll,** and **Oprah Winfrey,** in later sections of this book.

George Soros, the founder and chairman of the **Open Society Foundations**, draws upon his experiences growing up in Hungary, with furious conflicts stirred up by fascism and communism, where he experienced anti-Semitism and other forms of intolerance. After he was able to come to the West and to make his fortune in finance, he concentrated on providing opportunities for open societies in the former Soviet Union from the early 1990s. He established the **Central European University** in 1991 and the **Open Society Institute** in 1993. During the next three decades, he gave over $8 billion to foundations promoting democratic institutions in the US, Africa, Asia, Europe, and Latin America. He has long been dedicated to supporting human rights, freedom of expression, and opportunities for public health and education in seventy countries (www.soros.org).

Eli Broad, who is the founding chairman of KB Home Corporation in homebuilding and Sun America in retirement savings services, and his wife, **Edythe,** have established the **Broad Foundation** in Los Angeles. Their mission is to transform "K-12 urban public education through better governance, management, labor relations and competition." They are also contributing to advance significant scientific and medical research. In addition, they are increasing global access to contemporary art. They are giving substantial support to Los Angeles civic projects as well (www.broadfoundation.org). Some recent grants in education include supporting public schools in Washington, D.C., the **Harvard University Education Innovation Laboratory,** the **Broad Prize for Urban Education** established in 2002, and the **Los Angeles Inner City Education Foundation** for charter schools and schools in other communities.[8] At the same time, they have been sponsoring scientific and medical research on genomics, stem cells, regenerative medicine, and other fields at Harvard and MIT, UCSF, USC, UCLA, and other universities. In the arts, they established the **Broad Contemporary Art Museum at the Los Angeles County Museum of Art,** which opened in 2008, to showcase art from 1945 onward. They have also become a vast contemporary art lending resource. (www.broadartfoundation.org)

Michael Bloomberg has followed a substantial business career in information technology with three terms as mayor of New York City and mega-giving through the **Bloomberg Philanthropies.** Among his outstanding donations has been the **Bloomberg School of Public Health at Johns Hopkins University,** which is the world's largest school of its kind centered on improving health and preventing disease and disability. It also has an outstanding Malaria Research institute.

Major Bloomberg has been supporting education, the arts, health, and environmental and social service organizations not only in New York and other American cities, but also around the globe, with total donations of more than $1.6 billion by 2011 to over one thousand charities (www.mikebloomberg.com; www.bloomberg.com) An example of his innovative approach is **Young Men's Initiative,** a program he launched in 2011 to create educational and job possibilities for NYC's black and Latino men. The unusual funding will come from both private and public sources. He has pledged $30 million, which will be matched by **George Soros;** the city will pay the remaining costs of around $67 million.[9]

Ted Turner, who chairs turner Enterprises, created CNN, and was former vice chair of Time Warner Inc., is a master at capturing attention for the causes he believes in. For example, when he pledged $1 billion in 1997 to form the **United Nations Foundation,** it was considered the largest private donation until that time. The UN Foundation has been mobilizing energy and expertise from both business and non-profit sectors to help the UN deal with major challenges like climate change, global health, peace and security, women's empowerment, poverty eradication, energy access, and US-UN relations (www.unfoundation.org) In addition, Ted Turner created and chairs the **Turner Foundation** to focus on environmental issues, such as improving air and water quality, developing a sustainable energy future, and wildlife habitat protection. He also supports the **Nuclear Threat Initiative,** which works to reduce global threats from nuclear, biological, and chemical weapons (www.tedturner.com). When Ted Turner spoke at the New York Public Library (NYPL) on May 4, 2011, he said that to give, you don't have to have a lot of money. All you need is love and a plan. He gave **Big Brothers and Big Sisters** as an example of the kind of organization to join and encouraged semiretired people to be active in social work.

Jon M. Huntsman, Sr., who made his fortune in chemicals and is a four-time cancer survivor, has contributed to combating cancer through the **Huntsman Cancer Institute at the University of Utah.** In addition, he has also emphasized education by contributing generously to the University of Pennsylvania's Wharton School, Utah State University's business school, and fifteen hundred college scholarships. Since he himself believes strongly in helping others, when Warren Buffet invited him in 2009 to sign the Giving Pledge to donate 50 percent of his wealth, he told him, "You don't have the formula right. It should be eight percent."[10]

Even people who can give million to a cause still have to plan their campaigns and donations very carefully to get measurable results, according to **Peter B Lewis,** a generous billionaire who takes a very active role in his philanthropies. He believes, he said at the NYPL on May 4, 2011, that philanthropy should be treated like a business: you have to have clear goals expressed in a mission statement and make clear to the people working for you exactly what you expect from them. He amplified his views in response to my question during his talk at the Princeton Club on May 25, 2011, by saying he believes in focus and precision in both business and philanthropy in order to deliver results. Lewis, who made his fortune in auto insurance, is the largest contributor to **Princeton University,** since he gave his alma mater over $220 million. This included the biggest gift in Princeton's history: $101 million for the creative and performing arts.[11] Since he has strong ideas about the directions the institutions receiving his donations should take, when he disagrees with the then-director of the **Guggenheim Museum** in New York, Thomas Kerns, he resigned as chairman of the museum board. Lewis also contributes to the American Civil Liberties Union, the Center for American Progress, and other progressive causes. Lewis explained his approach to giving is that "something has to grab me emotionally, and I have to be convinced that the money I gave them will turn out to do what they say they want to do with it, and… I want to have fun with it."[12]

Jeffrey "Jeff" Bezos, who started and developed Amazon.com into the world's dominant online retailer and also a Princeton alumnus, gave $10 million to the **Museum of History & Industry in Seattle** to found a "Center for innovation" at the museum's new location. In explaining his gift, Bezos said, "Look at the disproportionate number of extraordinary organizations founded in Seattle Microsoft Costco, Boeing… even UPS was founded here… These companies and their innovations have had a big impact on Seattle, the country and the world."[13]

Mark Zuckerberg, one of the world's youngest billionaires through co-founding Facebook, pledged $100 million at the end of 2010 to found his **Startup: Education Foundation** to assist public schools in Newark, New Jersey, and around the country. He aims to improve national education.[14] "People wait until late in their careers to give back," he said. "But why wait when there is so much to be done? With a generation of younger folks who have thrived on the success of their companies, there is a big opportunity for many of us to give back earlier in our lifetime and see the impact of our philanthropic efforts."[15]

Just as Bill and Melinda Gates and Warren Buffet have inspired other billionaires to pledge at least 50 percent of their fortunes during their lifetimes, they have also set an example for every one of us to give as much as we can to help others in the most constructive ways possible.

* * *

B. INNOVATIVE GIVERS FOR MEANINGFUL CAUSES

Passion adds so much to giving when it reflects the actions of people who have done well for themselves and want to give back to others. Then there are people who have suffered from a disease or who have known afflicted people and who then want to conquer the disease and improve conditions for the sufferers. Many other people devote themselves passionately to causes they feel have the highest priority.

Charles F. ("Chuck") Feeney, an Irish-American businessman, grew up modest circumstances in New Jersey, but went on to make a fortune through Duty Free Shops. He donated anonymously as long as he could and then gave publically through the **Atlantic Philanthropies** (AP) he established in 1982. He has used his business profits to bring about "lasting changes in the lives of disadvantaged and vulnerable people." With the goal of "Giving While Living," the foundation has been supporting programs for the aging, youth, human rights, poverty, and health in the US, Australia, Ireland, South Africa, and elsewhere. It gave $600 million to Feeney's alma mater, **Cornell University**, mainly for financial aid to students. Then in 2011, AP gave an additional $350 million to Cornell to build a new high-tech graduate school for applied sciences in New York City in conjunction with **Technion-Israel Institute of Technology.** "This is a once-in-a-generation opportunity," Mr. Feeney said, "to create economic and educational opportunities on a transformational scale."[1]

AP is the single largest funder of comprehensive immigration reform in the US. AP made grants for over $5.5 billion by 2010 and expects by 2020 to become the largest foundation in history to spend down its endowment. Meanwhile, Feeney himself continues to live modestly and does not even own a home or a car. He continues to travel extensively – in economy class. He explained his motives in his biography, *The Billionaire Who Wasn't*: "I had no idea that never changed in my mind – that you should use your wealth to help people" (www.atlanticphilanthropies.org). He offers a perfect example of someone who derives the greatest pleasure from giving to others.

The **Robin Hood Foundation,** which was founded in 1988 by hedge fund manager **Paul Tudor Jones** and other financial leaders, is a prime practitioner of venture philanthropy by applying investment principles to reduce poverty. It works with more than two hundred New York City poverty-fighting nonprofit organizations in such fields as early childhood, education, jobs, and survival through program and capital grants and funds to build management capacity. Their approach is to give 100 percent of the money raised to their programs. The administrative expenses for the staff and their gala fundraising events are contributed by board members. The foundation seeks the best returns through evaluating and measuring the results (www.robinhood.org). The board members include **George Soros**, who gave $50 million in 2009, and other Wall Street figures, many whom are listed in the 2011 Forbes 400, as well as leading entertainers, including **Lady Gaga**, who often appear at the annual galas. The

2010 gala in May raised a record setting $88 million,[2] while the 2011 reached $47 million during more difficult times.

Another remarkable donor is **J. K. Rowling**, who went from being a single parent on welfare to becoming a billionaire through the **Harry Potter** books and films. Beginning in 2000, she has been giving back to overcome problems she has encountered personally, especially to the **Volant Charitable Trust,** which uses its annual budget of 5.1 million British pounds to combat poverty and social inequality, the trust also contributes to organizations that aid children, one-parent families, and multiple sclerosis research. Rowling said, "I think you have a moral responsibility when you've been given far more than you need, to do wise things with it and give intelligently."[3] She has become president of the charity **One Parent Families**. In addition, since her mother died from multiple sclerosis, she has given money and support for the research and treatment of this disease. She has also contributed substantially for the creation of the **Centre for Regenerative Medicine at Edinburgh University.** Another benefit of the worldwide fascination with Harry Potter has been encouraging children to read more.

Sandra Lee, who has a large following for her TV show on the Food Network and has written twenty-two cookbooks so far, has been helping hungry children because she was once one of them. As she was growing up in a poor household, she became active with **Share Our Strength** and food banks around the country.

Share Our Strength, which was founded in 1984 by brother and sister **Bill and Debbie Shore** to end childhood hunger in America, is dedicated to improving the access families all over the country have to healthy, affordable food. They are working at the state and city level with the help of government, corporations, and volunteers on a "No Kid Hungry" campaign (www.strength.org).

Reginald F. Lewis, an African-American Harvard Law School graduate, went on to serve as chairman of TLC Beatrice International Holdings Corp. until his death in 1993. His foundation continues the fellowship programs he established while he was alive to promote diversity at **Harvard Law School**. His widow, **Loida Lewis**, who heads the foundation, said he wanted "black students to walk a little taller and work a little harder." They have also supported the **Reginald**

L. Lewis Museum of Maryland African-American History and Culture in Baltimore.[5]

The **Make-A-Which Foundation** has been granting the "wishes of children with life-threatening medical conditions to enrich the human experience with hope. Strength and joy" since 1980. They had reached over two hundred and fifty thousand children around the world by 2011 with the help of a network of about twenty-five thousand volunteers, as well as donors, sponsors, and staff members. The foundation president. **David Williams**, said they granted the wishes of 13,580 children in fiscal 2010, the most ever in a single year (www.wish.org).

So many individuals have been using their imagination and experience to help others. For example, **Ruth Lande Shuman** is the founder and president of **Publicolor**, which goes into NYC school to get disaffected students to paint the public areas in their schools with bright colors to make dreary interiors come alive and to feel they can affect their learning environment. As they participate in the design and painting process with the nonprofit's volunteers and staff, they become proud of their schools and eager to attend classes. Then they have opportunities to learn and enjoy themselves through club activities, mentoring, and reading and writing, as well as career training (www.publicolor.org).

Pam Allyn is executive director of **LitWorld**, an international literacy organization that aims to teach one million children to read by 2014 through training literacy leaders all over the world. In its first few years, the organization had worked in thirty-five countries and reached forty thousand people. One of its main projects has been reading clubs for girls from Iraq to Liberia to Kenya (www.litworld.org).[6]

Each of us can encourage literacy and love for learning in children through our local libraries. For example, **Arnold and Arlene Goldstein**, who are in their seventies, have contributed $600,000 to the **New York Public Library** for a teen center at the Hamilton Grange Library in Harlem because they want to provide opportunities for children that they enjoyed when they were growing up.[7]

Another imaginative program is the **Ghetto Film School in the Bronx**, which nurtures future directors, producers, set designers, and others aiming at the entertainment industry. **Joe Hall**, a former

Bronx social worker and film student founded the school in 2000 and has been producing videos and other projects with over one hundred and thirty alumni in its first decade. The program includes international travel for film shoots to broaden career vistas.[8]

After **Petra Nemcova**, a model, was injured in Thailand by the 2004 Indian Ocean tsunami and had recovered, she started **Happy Hearts Fund** in 2005 to rebuild lives for children affected by natural disasters. She especially wanted to cover the period between the first response and government relief programs. The fund provides for administrative costs to be covered by corporations so that 100 percent of all donations could directly go to the children in need. Projects have been underway in Hurricane Katrina-affected US locations, as well as in Thailand, Indonesia, Mexico, India, and other countries to build schools and help children and community members (www.happyheartsfund.org).

Some people have very specific priorities. For example, **Jon L. Stryker**, an architect who is heir to a medical products company fortune, gave $30.8 million in 2010 to the **Arcus Foundation**, which he founded in 2000. This way following even larger contributions he had made from 2006-2009. The Arcus Foundation works to advance gay, lesbian, bisexual, and transgender equality, and to conserve and protect the great apes (www.arcusfoundation.org).[9]

There is nothing like laughter to soothe pain so the **Friars Club**, so many of whose members are famous comedians, started the **Gift of Laughter Wounded Warriors Program** in 2007 to help wounded veterans of the Iraq and Afghanistan campaigns recover physically and mentally (www.giftoflaughter.org; www.woundedwarriorproject.org). One of the major supporters of the program is member **Jim O'Donnell**, who said it is a responsibility to give back to those who served in the two conflicts. He wants "to help those that have given so much to us."[10]

People who help others offer wonderful examples of how their vision and passions motivate them to undertake serious commitments through existing organizations and institutions and through creating new structures.

* * *

C. SOCIAL ENTREPRENEURS WHO STRIVE FOR IMPACT

How can you maximize the impact of your contributions in a practical way for the causes you believe in? The social entrepreneurship approach is to apply business methods and management techniques to investments and enterprises. The entrepreneur should set goals, invest both to make a profit and to help society, create and sustain efficient, effective institutions, and then measure and evaluate the results. Finally, it is possible to apply the findings to readjust the investment portfolio or enterprise.

A leading proponent of social entrepreneurship is **Pierre Omidyar,** who founded the online auction company **eBay** in 1995. In 2004, he and his wife, **Pam,** established the **Omidyar Network,** "which makes investments in for-profit companies as well as grants to nonprofits organizations, with social impact being the unifying criterion for investment" (www.omidyar.com). Pierre Omidyar said the "idea of giving away lots of money is much more difficult than it sounds if you care about the impact this money is going to have. "He added that 'it's really fun... There are a lot of opportunities ...to find the synergies between the nonprofit approaches to a problem and the for-profit... and market-based approaches to that problem. "Examples of what he has been doing include government transparency with the **Sunlight Foundation** and greater access to public information through **Code for America.**[1]

The Omidyar have already given more than $1 billion in donations. For example, in 2010, they gave $61.5 million to the Omidyar Network; Hope Lab, a California nonprofit that Ms. Omidyar chairs to develop technology for chronically ill children; and other groups.[2] They also established the **Omidyar-Tufts Microfinance Fund** at Tufts University in 2005 with a $100 million gift to be invested entirely in international microfinance initiatives.

Jeff Skoll, the first president of the eBay, founded the **Skoll foundation** in 1999. Which soon became the world's largest foundation for social entrepreneurship. The goal has been to bring about "large-scale change by investing in, connecting, and celebrating social entrepreneurs and other innovators dedicated to solving the world's most pressing problems." The foundation supports the **Skoll Awards for Social Entrepreneurship,** given by 2011 to eighty-five leading social entrepreneurs supporting the neediest populations in over one hundred countries (www.skollfoundation.org).

An important influence on both Omidyar and Skoll has come from **Bill Drayton,** who founded **Ashoka** in 1978 to find and encourage entrepreneurship worldwide through supporting thousands of fellows in more than sixty countries with funds contributed by foundations, especially through the Omidyar's. Other people and institutions most active in giving seed capital and advice for social entrepreneurs through Bill Drayton include **Chuck Freeney**, the **Mac Arthur Fellowship,** the **Rockefeller Brothers Fund,** and the **Rockefeller Foundation.** A major European backer, **Stephan Schmidheiny** from Switzerland, has supported Ashoka in its Latin American programs.[3]

Another prime exponent of social entrepreneurship is **Google. org**, which is committed to using its expertise in information and technology to build engineering and the other projects that address global challenges, such as climate change, clean energy, and global health. When Google went public in 2004, its founders, **Sergey Brin** and **Larry Page,** pledged to reserve one percent of its profit and equity to "make the world a better place,"[4] In 2010, they gave more than $184 million to nonprofits, academic institutions, and other grants. They have been sponsoring engineering and other academic research, especially through **Google RISE Awards** (roots in science and engineering) and many innovative projects. In addition, they have been providing scholarship, especially to women and minorities, in computer science and technology. They have also been donating in kind products, such as videos and Google Earth and Maps, and encouraging volunteerism among their employees (www.google.org).

Social entrepreneurship, also called venture philanthropy, has been evolving with ideas and techniques from venture capital finance and high technology business management. It has been analyzed most thoroughly in Bishop and Green's *Philanthrocapitalism: How Giving Can Save the World.*[5]

The central goal of social entrepreneurship is to build self-sustaining social ventures that include nonprofit and profit-making companies. New types of legal hybrids like **low-profit limited liability companies (LC3s),** which have a triple bottom line-people, planet, and profits- have also been developed.[6]

About five hundred chief executives, company founders, nonprofit leaders, and investor have come together in the **Social Venture Network,** which "connects, supports and inspires business leaders and social entrepreneurs in expanding practices that build a just sustainable economy" (www.svn.org).

Acumen fund exemplifies the approach of substituting self-reliance strategies in place of charity. This enterprising organization, which is committed to finding ways to give poor people dignity and the ability to take care of themselves rather than gifts, was incorporated in 2001 with seed capital from the Rockefeller Foundation and other groups. **Jacqueline Novogratz** initiated the fund to change the way the world tackles poverty. Their vision is to invest in social enterprises, emerging leaders, and breakthrough ideas by offering critical services-water, heath, housing, and energy-at affordable prices to people earning less than four dollars a day. In their first ten years, Acumen fund reports they invested $60 million in fifty-seven enterprises with thirty-five thousand workers, affecting forty million people. They have been doing this through offices and programs in New York, India, Pakistan, and East and West Africa. In each project, they encourage local leadership and funding (www.acumenfund.org).[7]

Harold Schultz, chairman and CEO of **Starbucks**, combined business and philanthropy in 2011 when he started "Create Jobs for USA." A grass-roots private fund to make loans to small businesses in underserved markets through the country. Customers at the sixty-seven hundred company-owned US stores can buy a special five-dollar red, white, and blue wristband that says "indivisible." All the money raised will go to the nonprofit **Opportunity Finance Network,** which backs one hundred and eighty community financial institutions. Other funds will be coming from the bracelets (one hundred thousand were sold in the first few days they became available), the **Starbucks Foundation,** and Schultz and his wife, **Sheri.**[8]

Laurene Powell Jobs, widow of **Steve Jobs**, has been active in education reform, especially in **College Track**, which she co-founded in 1997 to help low-income students prepare for college with the help of both academic and extra-curricular programs. She is also established a philanthropic organization called the **Emerson Collective**, which stresses self-reliance and works with "a range of entrepreneurs to advance domestic and international social reform efforts."[9] She is also an active supporter of the nonprofit **Global Fund for Women**, which supports local initiatives to improve women's health and education internationally.[10]

On a practical level, many new M.B.A.s are combining careers in nonprofit and for-profits enterprises in order to assure themselves financial security while contributing to needy causes. While only three percent of Harvard Business School's Social Enterprise Initiative accepted jobs in 2011 in the nonprofit and government sectors, others have found private-sector jobs that deal with global poverty, environmental or sustainability concerns, or other social issues. Some graduates of other business schools are taking private-sector jobs initially to get experience and then working for nonprofit organizations.[11]

More than twelve million Americans from forty-four to seventy years old have indicated they want to start nonprofits or businesses that solve social problems, according to a study by **Civil Ventures**, a San Francisco think tank. The study, which was supported by the **MetLife Foundation** and put together by the marketing research firm **Penn Schoen Berland**, also reports that more than half of these twelve million people believe they will really start such an enterprise within the next five to ten years.[12]

Trends show that many social entrepreneurship entities have been growing by applying good business practices to work and invest in socially desirable enterprises that can be self-supporting and encourage self-reliance for people who never had such opportunities before.

* * *

D. CELEBRITIES WHO PROMOTE GIVING TO OTHERS

Bill Clinton, Paul Newman, Oprah Winfrey, and other celebrities lend their names resources to helping others in imaginative ways and inspire others to emulate them. They use their enormous media impact to galvanize people for the causes they advocate.

President Bill Clinton has forcefully promoted **Clinton Global Initiatives** since 2005 to improve the lives of more than two hundred million people in over one hundred and seventy countries. The **William J. Clinton Foundation** has been focusing on economic empowerment, education, environment and energy, health systems, and nutrition. In all their initiatives, they emphasize partnership and collaboration, measurable results, innovation and markets, efficiency and sustainability, replication, and scale, as well as systematic change and local impact (www.clintonfoundation.org). Bill Clinton communicates his ideas enthusiastically in his book called *Giving: How Each of Us Can Change the World.*[1]

Paul Newman contributed to children, health, hunger, human rights, literacy, the environment, and many other causes by giving 100 percent of the proceeds after taxes from his salad dressings and other food and beverages through his **Newman's Own Foundation** to thousands of charities around the world. His guiding principles ranged from "Let's give it all away" to "The need is great and so are the opportunities to make a difference. "Since his death in 2008 from lung cancer, the foundation has been continuing his work and had given more than given more than $300 million by 2011 (www.newmansownfoundation.org).

Oprah Winfrey, the talk show host and entertainment dynamo. Has been contributing to children, education, and other causes in America and abroad through her **Angel Network** founded in 2000, in conjunction with the **Boys and Girls Clubs of America, UNICEF,** and other organizations. The Angel Network, with Free the **Free the Children,** had built fifty-five schools in twelve countries by 2011. It also used **Oprah's Book Club Awards** as the basis for providing book in region where the books are based, such as China for pearl Buck's

The Good Earth (www.oprahsangelnetwork.org). In recognition of her philanthropic contributions, including over $500 million of her own money, the Academy of Motion Picture Arts and Sciences chose her for one of its three Humanitarian Awards in 2011.[2] She has said, "Think about what you have to give not in terms of dollars, because I believe that your life is about service."[3]

Michael J. Fox, who had a very successful acting career, revealed in 1998 that he had been suffering from Parkinson's Disease for seven years and wanted to devote himself to the campaign for more research about the disease. His **Michael J. Fox Foundation** for Parkinson's Research is dedicated both to finding a cure and developing improved therapies for people afflicted with the disease (www.michaeljfox.org).

Bono (Paul David Hewson), the Irish singer, has aroused enormous public support for his causes, such as third-world debt relief, hunger and AIDS, especially in Africa. He has organized many benefit concerts and received recognition from Presidents Clinton and George W. Bush and many other world leaders.

Angelina Jolie, the movie actress, became concerned about humanitarian problems while she was filming *Lora Croft: Tomb Raider* (2001) in Colombia, which influenced her to visit refugee camps in that country and others. This led to her appointment as a Goodwill Ambassador for the **United Nations High Commissioner for Refugees** (UNHCR) in 2001. She has continued to visit refugee camps and bring regions, such as Iraq, Afghanistan, and Dafur. She had drawn attention to their plight and has helped to publicize World Refugee Day.[4]

Celebrities can focus attention on major problems and help raise funds to alleviate or solve them. The also perform a great service by inspiring others.

* * *

E. GOVERNMENT OFFICIALS AND NONPROFIT PROFESSIONALS

Many people feel that they can accomplish most benefit society by tracking major challenges through government service and nonprofit organizations. **President John F. Kennedy's** inspiring call from his 1961 inaugural still echoes: "Ask not what your country can do for you – ask what you can do for your country."

Some serious government and nonprofit leaders come to their positions after having made fortunes in business or finance, such as **Mayor Michael Bloomberg** in New York, or inherited great wealth, such as President Kennedy or **Governor Nelson Rockefeller** in New York and **Governor Winthrop Rockefeller** in Arkansas. Most outstanding public and nonprofit sector leaders choose their careers based upon their convictions and concepts of how they can have the greatest impact. For example, my nephew, **Andre Gruber**, left a promising position with a major law firm to become the general counsel for the Chicago Regional Transportation Authority and then moved to Salt Lake City to become the executive director of the Wasatch Front Regional Council, Utah. "Contributing large sums of money to well-known charities is not the only way to give," he feels. "Executives in the government and nonprofit sectors often sacrifice private-sector compensation levels but have other opportunities to make contributions. As a government executive, I look for opportunities to partner with charities by providing data, specialized experience and training, and even regulatory or legislative advocacy, there are also opportunities to structure government grant or loan programs to reward or leverage private charitable efforts. All it takes is a commitment to promoting charitable endeavors and a little creativity."[1]

Selected examples of what is being done include government officials who are renown for their effectiveness and probity, and others directing national and international programs; foundation heads; university officials; heads of cultural institutions; and leaders of organizations concentrating on helping less advantaged people. While space is limited these individuals represent multitudes of dedicated people at all levels who are giving to others locally, nationally, and internationally.

The model for government prosecutors nationwide is undoubtedly **Robert M. Morgenthau**, who served as **Manhattan district attorney** from 1975 until his retirement in 2009. He was the third generation of his family in public service. His father, **Henry Morgenthau, Sr.**, was US ambassador to the Ottoman Empire under President Woodrow Wilson. Before his diplomatic career, he had made a fortune in real estate.

Robert Morgenthau had always considered going into government service, but when he was in the US Navy in 1944, his ship was torpedoed off Algiers. He later told CNN that while "I was floating around in the water, I made promises to the Almighty." This led him to study law at Yale and then go into practice. He devoted considerable time and effort to community organizations and campaigned for John F. Kennedy in 1960. He accepted an appointment as United States attorney for the Southern District of New York. Thereafter, he was in private practice for four and a half years. He then ran for and was elected to the office of district attorney of New York County.

As a very dynamic and accomplished Manhattan district attorney. He expanded his office to thirty-four bureaus and units, specializing in a wide range of fields, including labor racketeering, money laundering, Asian gangs, sex crimes, and elder abuse. His office provided a model for many others around the country. He was so highly regarded that for thirty-five years he was generally returned to office unopposed, except for two contests.[2] Despite his official duties, he has found time to support nonprofit organizations, such as the police Athletic League. In addition, he has been the long-serving chairman of the museum of Jewish Heritage- A living memorial to the Holocaust in New York.

A prime example of a person bringing new energy to a bureaucratic organization is **Dr. Raj Shah,** who led many campaigns, including distributing vaccines, during the decade he spent at the Gates Foundation. From there, President Obama chose him at thirty-eight to head **USAID** in Washington and to revitalize the American foreign aid program. Shah indicated in a *Fortune* interview, "In order to really solve problems… you have to break them down to their most transparent and simple pieces. "He is also applying the Gates precedent of thinking on a massive scale. At the same time, he prefers not rely just on contractors, but to use social media to reach individuals all over Africa and Asia. In addition, he is encouraging people in the field to buy locally whenever possible.[3]

Long before the Gates Foundation was started, two other wealthy benefactors established foundations that the other evolved in ways their original founders would probably not have imagined: the **Rockefeller Foundation** in 1913 and the **Form Foundation in 1936. The Ford Founding in 1936.** The directions they have been taking have depended upon their guiding Leadership. **Dr. Judith Rodin**, president of the Rockefeller Foundation since 2005, from example, has found ways to revitalize its mission of promoting the well-being of humanity. The emphasis is on innovative solutions to the challenges of globalization and resilience to counter risks. They strive to create leverage not only with their dollars, but also with their extensive experience, expertise, and convening power. Dr. Rodin, the first woman to head an Ivy League institution as president of the University of Pennsylvania. During the decade she spent at Penn, she expanded university research and general facilities enormously, and led a comprehensive neighborhood revitalization program (www. rockefellerfoundation.org).

Luis A. Ubinas, Ford Foundation president since 2008, brings a background in technology, telecommunications, and media, which he has used to enhance the way nonprofits deliver results for the people served, including those from poor and marginalized communities. The Ford Foundation "supports visionary leaders and organizations on the frontlines of social change worldwide." Its continuing goals have been to strengthen democratic values, reduce poverty and injustice, promote international cooperation, and advance human achievement through collaboration among the nonprofit, government, and business sectors and other means (www. fordfoundation.org).

Every cultural institution needs a visionary leader with multiple skills to revitalize the existing collections and programs as times change and to attract increased support in order to survive. **Susan Henshaw Jones,** the president and director of the **Museum of the City of New York (MCNY),** has been a rescuer of museums, beginning with the **National Building Museum** in Washington, D.C. in the 1990s. She took over the MCNY in 2003 and then added the presidency of the **South Street Seaport Museum** in 2011. **Kate D. Levin**, the NYC Commissioner of Cultural Affairs, called upon her to add the second institution because of her managerial skills and innovative approaches. "She gets result," Ms. Levin said. "She knows how to take history off the walls and make it come alive."[4]

Dr. Anthony W. Marx, president of the New York Public Library (NYPL) since 2011, has been devoted to offering "equal access to knowledge for all" throughout his career. He fought for change in South Africa in the 1980s before and after Princeton graduate school, and helped to found a South African secondary school to prepare more than one thousand black students to attend white universities. As a political science professor at Columbia, Dr. Marx founded a program to recruit graduate students to teach in low-income public schools. Following his earlier pattern, he created a number of high schools linked to universities to enable low-income students to attend college. When he was **Amherst president** for eight years beginning in 2003, he transformed the college's admissions policies to recruit more low-income and minority students. As NYPL president since 2011, he has emphasized expanding library programs and services for "the full range of citizens, youngest learning to read, scholars of all types, and the elderly."[5]

Since the library has always been in the forefront of giving opportunities to talented immigrants and citizens, he said, "The need for that is even greater today, even as the technology forces us to rethink how we deliver that opportunity."[6]

Dr. Susan Desmond-Hellmann, a medical doctor and a successful pharmaceutical entrepreneur at Genentech, has become chancellor of the University of California, San Francisco, where she studied medicine and met her husband. Instead of becoming a wealthy retiree, she and her husband, Dr. Nicholas Hellmann, gave $1 million to the university, and she became chancellor at fifty-two in 2009. Scientists know the San Francisco campus as a leader in biomedical research and innovation. Despite constrictions in the national economy and the university with twenty-three thousand employees, two hospital complexes, and numerous clinics, students, residents, and postdoctoral fellows. Her vision for the university is to make it "the world's pre-eminent health sciences innovator." This includes "unparalleled" patient care, top faculty and stall, and rapid movement from scientific discoveries into treatments.[7]

Scott Syphax is the president and CEO of **Nehemiah Corporation of America (NCA).** One of the largest nonprofit community development organizations in the country. Under his leadership, NCA, which was founded in Sacramento, California, in 1994, has created over two hundred thousand new homeowners by providing more than $800 million in down-payment assistance gifts. It has also formed a partnership with the US Conference of Mayors to develop viable solutions for affordable homeownership, according to the Sacramento Entrepreneurship Academy (www.sealink.org).

At the same time, Syphax is the chair of the board of governors of **CORO**, a thirty-year-old nonprofit that trains leaders in public service. Coro provides opportunities for its midcareer fellows to rotate among private, government, nonprofit, and policy organizations in New York, San Francisco, Los Angeles, Cleveland, and other locations where it is based to "really understand how policy and decision-making work," according to Scott Millstein, executive director of NY Coro.[8] Over ten thousand Coro alumni are serving currently as leaders in local, regional, and national global businesses, nonprofit organizations, governmental agencies, and elected public office. Among the alumni are Scott Syphax, **Senator Dianne Feinstein** (CA). **Iris Chen,** president and CEO of the **"I Have a Dream"** **Foundation**, which empowers children in low-income communities to pursue higher education, and many others (www.coro.org).

Allen Waxman, a lawyer in the Kaye Scholer firm, is also chair of the board of **Equal Justice Works**, a nonprofit in Washington that arranges opportunities for law students and lawyers to pursue careers representing underserved communities and causes. The organization runs the largest US postgraduate legal fellowship program working in civil rights, environmental. And human rights law, as well as defending victims of domestic defending victims of domestic violence and human trafficking. They also have a lawyer debt relief program to assist these public interest lawyers to pay off their student loans and therefore be able to afford the pursuit of pre bono law positions (www.equaljusticeworks.org)."9

Rosa W. Boone, executive director of the Westchester Coalition for the Hungry and Homeless, Inc., has been coordinating the activities of thirty-eight soup kitchens, seventy-two food pantries, and thirty-one shelters serving over two hundred and forty thousand people in Westchester Country, In addition to her professional staff, she has been attracting hundreds of volunteers and donors who want to assist in the struggle against hunger and homelessness (www. foodclothingshelter.org).

The astonishing range of creative initiatives cited here represents a wider spectrum of constructive activities by dedicated government officials and nonprofit professionals who give ideas, energy, basic funding when possible, and thoughtful, inspiring leadership to many people through they are contributing to our society in innumerable ways.

* * *

F. VOLUNTEERS WHO HELP IN MANY IMAGINATIVE WAYS

Volunteering is so central to the American way of life. It takes concern for others, imagination, and perseverance, but not money, so it is the easiest way to give for everyone. Yet something important s required-a lot of thought about how you can be most helpful. First choose the category where you want to help make a difference: hunger, less advantaged young people, schools. Hospitals, emergency situations, animals, the environment, and many more. Next consider the organizations and groups around you that could use you help, such as religious-affiliated organizations. Big Brothers and Big Sisters, neighborhood groups, etc., and find out how you can assist them and how much time and effort it would take. Once you have found activities to strengthen programs and help others.

In order to see the larger picture, let us consider American volunteering in general, an online directory for finding volunteer positions by location and sector, central government agencies running volunteer programs, some major volunteer opportunities, and then examples of individual volunteers.

About one-quarter of the American population has been volunteering annually. For example, around sixty-three million people age sixteen or older volunteered in 2010, including about 35 percent with religious groups, 27 percent with educational organizations, and 14 percent with social service groups. Around the country, Utah had the greatest number of volunteers, followed by Iowa, Minnesota, Nebraska, and South Dakota. By age group, the greatest number came from those in their thirties and early to mid-forties. Next came the baby boomers (those in their late forties or older), and then those in their twenties.[1]

If you want a broad range of choices, go to www.volunteer.match.org and check out the possibilities by location and institution put of the more than seventy-nine thousand nonprofit organizations listed. They have made almost six million referrals from 1998 to 2011.

AmeriCorps is comprehensive government agency offering about seventy-five thousand opportunities for community service on the national and state levels to tutor and mentor disadvantaged youth, fight illiteracy, build affordable housing, clean parks and streams, and other services. In addition, it has a special AmeriCorps VISTA program to provide full-time capacity-builders to bring low-income individuals and communities out of poverty. The **AmeriCorps National Civilian Community Corps (NCCC)** is designed especially for full-time volunteers ages eighteen to twenty-four to strengthen communities while developing leaders. Full-time young volunteers who complete their service receive education awards to help pay college and graduate school expenses, and some AmeriCorps members may receive a modest living allowance while they are serving (www.americorps.gov).

The **HandsOn Network** is the largest American volunteer structure, with more than seventy thousand corporate, faith, and nonprofit organization programs to enlist volunteer service. As part of their outreach efforts, they provide AmeriCorps alums with more than one hundred and twenty thousand experienced volunteer leaders committed to lifelong improvement of their communities (www.handsonnetwork.org).

Among the outstanding volunteer organizations. **Big Brothers Big Sisters** has been supporting mentoring services for more than one hundred years to "provide children facing adversity with strong and enduring, professionally supported one-to-one relationships that change their lives for the better, forever" (www.bbbs.org).

Many other groups are working to improve school s, for example, **Project Appleseed,** which encourages parental involvement and engagement in public school (www.projectappleseed.org). it offers guidelines for public-school volunteering (www.ehow.com).

To assist at the next level of getting jobs and developing careers, the **National Academy Foundation (NAF)** provides employees of more than twenty-five hundred companies as volunteer mentors in class and the workplace in finance, hospitality and tourism, information technology, and engineering. The NAF, founded in 1982 by **Sanford I. Weill,** chairman emeritus of Citigroup, Inc., has grown to more than five hundred academies over most of the US (www.naf.org).

Operation HOPE works to bring economic empowerment to underserved communities, providing the "silver rights" advocated by Ambassador Andrew Young to help low-income Americans participate actively in the free-market economy. Volunteers teach the underserved people about banking, mortgages, starting their own businesses, and other financial skills (www.operationhope.org).

In order to get and keep a job, it is important for people starting out without advantages to "dress for success," with mentors to help them develop careers. Started in 1997 by Nancy Lublin, **Dress for Success** has already helped more than fifty thousand women a year in the US and other countries (www.dressforsuccess.org) a similar organization for men, **Career Gear**, was started in 1999 (www.careergear.org).

For those considering volunteer work, there are many websites offering practical advice, e.g., for hospital volunteers, a possibility is: www.howstuffworks.com/economics/volunteer/opportunities/volunteer-at-hostpital.

The American Association for Museum Volunteers brings together paid and unpaid museum staff who work together. It represents the over one million volunteers in all categories of museums (www.aamv.org).

Natural disasters, such as earthquakes, tornadoes, hurricanes, and floods, along with terror attacks, civil wars, and other political conflicts, lead to enormous destruction and displacement and create special opportunities for volunteers to assist governments and professional organizations, such as the **American Red Cross**. Many people contribute their services through religious groups and lots of others. For example, **Marteen and Wiley Blankenship**, a senior couple living in Alabama, immediately heeded a call to clean up damage from tornadoes in their state in 2011, after they had come to the aid of Hurricane Katrina in 2005 and other disasters as members if the **Southern Baptist Convention.** Their church has about ninety-five thousand members in the US trained to offer relief from natural disasters, which makes them the third-largest American disaster-relief organization after the **Red Cross** and the **Salvation Army.**[2]

Most volunteers offer their services without seeking recognition, but sometimes unusual circumstances bring them to wider attention. **Marion Salmon Hedges**, a real estate agent, by the time she was forty-seven in 2011, had spent her life taking care of her children, her incapacitated sister, battered women, the terminally ill, and many other. When she was buying large supply of Halloween candy in East Harlem to distribute from her town house in Manhattan in November, 2011, a shopping cart thrown from four floors above crushed her. It was a terrible misfortune for a woman who had always been volunteering at the Stanley M. Isaacs Neighborhood Center, the New York Junior League, and the Brick Presbyterian Church to suddenly be helpless. Her family and friends related many more acts of her kindness when interviewed by *The New York Times*, November 2,2011. Subsequently, she was recuperating with rehabilitation services.

The **Presidential Citizens Medal** for at least forty years has honored Americans who have "performed exemplary deeds of service for their country or their fellow citizens." Among the twelve people cited in 2011 were **Camilla Bloomquist** of Penn Yan, New York, who founded **Food for the Needy** and **Christmas for the Needy; Judith Broder** of Studio City, California, who created **The Soldiers Project** to meet the mental health needs of service members and returning veterans and their families; and **Dr. Margaret Martin** of Los Angeles,

California, who founded the **Harmony Project** to replace violence in children's live with music by providing instruments and tuition-free music lessons. **Roberto Perez** of Miami, Florida, is president of **Alfalit**, a nonprofit group fighting illiteracy from Africa to South America. The organization has assisted seven million people in twenty-two countries to learn to read (www.presidentialserviceawards.gov) .

Volunteers have been serving society in innumerable ways. If you want to feel the joy of helping others and to avoid the frustrations of a program that may not be run correctly, choose a project or an organization where you want to volunteer and then evaluate the experience. You can continue with the original project if you feel you are accomplishing what you have set out to do or, if you detect shortcomings, make suggestions for improvements. If the organization does not improve, you can always leave and apply your energies elsewhere. When you are sincere in your desire to be helpful, you can find many ways to make a difference.

* * *

G. SOCIAL MEDIA NETWOKERS FOR GOOD CAUSES

Networking through **Facebook, Twitter**, and other social media provides new opportunities for people who want to join together for a cause, project, or campaign. The goal of **Causes**, for example, is to stimulate more charitable giving through digital means. It was founded in 2007 by **Joe Green** and former Facebook president **Sean Parker** to use social media tools to link charities with actual and potential supporters and donors. in a few years after starting as one of the first services on Facebook, it has already connected with over one hundred million users. Since their website slogan is "Anyone can change the world," each person finds a list of categories to choose from and then opportunities to learn more about specific charities. Causes encourages people to request a birthday charitable donation rather than a gift, which has already led to contributions in the millions of

GIVING IS NOT JUST FOR THE VERY RICH

dollars. It has also been developing programs with supermarkets and corporations to encourage giving (www.causes.com).1

Groupon began in 2008 as part of a group action and fundraising platform named The Point (started in 2007). As Groupon went on to emphasize consumer deals, they started "**The G-Team**" to aid Groupon users to donate money to selected charities. Anyone can start a campaign to ask people to give money or to take action as a group, but the project can go forward only if the campaign hits a predetermined tipping point. Groupon, which was founded by CEO **Andrew Mason**, enable people to feel they can make a difference by working with others (www.thepoint.com, www.groupon.com).

Among the social networks that help charities to attract volunteers are **LinkedIn** and **VolunteerMatch**, with the goal of bringing together a community of nonprofit, volunteer, and business leaders dedicated to improving society.

Since young people use social media constantly, **Do Something** was established by **Andrew Shue** and **Michael Sanchez** in 1993 to mobilize young people for civic activities. They wanted to "make community service as popular, cool, and most importantly, *normal*, as watching TV or playing sports..." The organization went mainly digital in 2003 under its new CEO, **Nancy Lublin**, who had founded Dress for Success. The group decided to focus on social changers twenty-five and under. By 2011, it was reaching about two million young people, through the web, television, mobile phones, and pop culture, who recognize the need to do something, believe they can do it, and then action (www.dosomething.org).

In a few years, so many social action and charitable networks have been formed that some of them have been merging. For example, **GOOD**, a publishing and marketing business that promotes social causes, acquired **Jumo**, a social network that raises funds and support for nonprofit groups, in 2011. GOOD, according to **Ben Goldhirsh**, its CEO and co-founder, announced from its beginning in 2006 that it was based on "pragmatism and idealism, creativity and impact" (www.good.is). GOOD's online magazine has an estimated three million visitors a month. It also raises revenues by working for profit with Starbucks, Pepsi and other corporations.[2]

Online giving has generally been increasing. According to **Network for Good**, a fundraising and volunteerism website, in 2001 only four percent of donors gave online. Ten years later about sixty-five percent of charitable giving was through the internet.[3] the **Blackbaud Index of Online Giving**, based on more than 1,780 nonprofit organizations totaling about $420 million a year, indicates that donations online generally increased from 4 to 15 percent a month, compared to the previous year in 2010-2011, but there were also some monthly decreases.[4]

Since online giving has been becoming more popular, it is important to find ways to regulate funds solicited on the social media. It is easiest with recognized **501(c) charities** that are listed and checked by **Charity Navigator** and other groups. New startups challenges, such as their authenticity, the amount collected actually going to the charity listed, and how long the money collected can be kept by the social media groups. State regulators have been trying hard to keep up with technologies to protect donors.[5]

* * *

III.

MAJOR AREAS FOR GIVING

A. RELIGIOUS PHILANTHROPY

Since religious philanthropy accounts for approximately one-third of all philanthropy in the US, it provides a convenient framework and base for giving of all kinds and at all levels. One can support schools, hospitals, and other institutions with money, time, and ideas, within one's chosen faith. Because one of the central premises of most religions is to help others, there are many local, national, and international choices within each religious group. You can focus on your local church, synagogue, or mosque, join national organizations, or reach out mainly abroad.

Personal experience within your own religious group is probably the best way to launch your giving. You can also find websites online that will broaden your awareness of what is available.

Let's start with Christian charities, beginning with the Catholics since they are the largest single religious group in America. Then we will go on to various Protestant denominations and to the Salvation Army. There is also much to consider among Moslem, Ismaili, Buddhist, and Hindu groups. Finally, we will turn to Jewish philanthropy, both religious and secular, for a more detailed analysis of the varieties of religious philanthropy.

CHRISTIAN CHARITIES

Catholic Charities U.S.A. states clearly on its website that it is working to reduce poverty in America. It is the national office for Catholic agencies and affiliates, while it supports local groups as they help over nine million people every year from many different religious, social, or economic backgrounds (www.catholiccharitiesusa.org). Many great universities, such as **Georgetown** and **Fordham,** are sponsored by Catholic groups. In addition, many Catholic orders provide elementary and secondary schools, health care facilities, and many more services.

The **Southern Baptist Convention** (SBC) is the largest Protestant denomination in the US (www.sbc.net). They emphasize their **World Hunger Fund,** which uses 100 percent of all monies received to feed people since they already have staff available globally to administer their programs (www.worldhungerfund.com). The SBC is the largest Baptist group in the world and is in turn part of the **Baptist World Alliance (BWA).** Charity Choice of BWA has programs worldwide to help the hungry, refugees, and victims of natural and man-made disasters and war, whether they are part of their groups or not. Their website offers suggestions about helping people in their own community and how to volunteer, as well as being transparent about their budget for programs and administration (www.charitychoices.com).

The **United Methodist Church,** the largest Mainline Protestant denomination and the third-largest Christian denomination after the Catholics and the Baptist, has been bringing together the mainline and evangelical branches since 1968. The Methodists have substantial educational institutions, such as **Wesleyan Universities** in New York, Ohio, Illinois, Texas, and elsewhere. The well-known **Wesleyan University in Connecticut** was founded by Methodists, but has become non-sectarian. The Methodists also have a whole array of charities. They believe in church-wide giving, which means that a portion of the contributions a person makes to a local church is used for regional, national, and international programs. For example, they are concerned with historically black colleges and African universities (www.umc.org).

Although churches like to present a harmonious front, somethings doctrinal differences about social and other issues lead to fissures. A prominent example is the dissension within the Lutheran Church between conservatives and liberals over Bible and homosexuality, which is affecting their extensive US social service programs.[1]

Each church seems to have its own service network, from the **Episcopalians** (www.episcopalcharities.org) to the **Unitarian Universalist Service Committee** (www.uusc.org) to the **Church of Latter Day Saints** (ldsphilanthropies.org) to the **Greek Orthodox** (www.iocc.org), and many, many more.

Many of the churches, Protestant, Anglican, Orthodox, Evangelical, Historic African-American, and others, have been coming together to discuss issues and programs in the **National Council of Churches** since its founding in 1950. Interfaith activities are also encouraged with Catholics, Jews, Moslems, Buddhists, and other religious group (www.nccusa.org). In turn, many of these faiths are also joined in the **World Council of Churched** (www.oikoumene.org).

One of the most prominent faith-based charities is the **Salvation Army**, originally started by **William Booth** in England in 1852. Its American activities, funded by street and online contributions, thrift stores, and other means, service poor and elderly people and help to rebuild lives for prisoners, drug and alcohol addicts, and others. The Salvation Army asserts it helped more than thirty million people in 2008 (www.salvationarmyusa.org).

Ten major Christian non-profits joined together in 2011 to end extreme poverty. Their leader is **Scott Todd**, a senior adviser at **Compassion International**, who wants to call upon the 138 million Christian living in the US to help the 1.4 billion people in the world existing in serious poverty.[2] Compassion International is a Christian child advocacy ministry to relieve children from spiritual, economic, social, and physical poverty so that they can become responsible, fulfilled Christian adults (www.compassion.com).

ISLAMIC CHARITIES

Islam emphasizes helping others locally, nationally, and internationally. The six top Islamic charitable organizations in the US, according to www.islam.about.com, include the following: **Islamic Relief**, which is concerned with international development relief activities and works from permanent offices in thirty-five countries as a partner with other international aid organizations, church group, and local relief agencies. **Life for Relief and Development** (LIFE) was founded by Iraqi American professionals in 1992 and provides humanitarian aid to people in Iraq. Afghanistan, and other Arab and Moslem countries. Another agency combating poverty is called **Muslim Aid**. Moslems are also active in the International Federation of Red Cross and Red Crescent Societies in many countries. The

Islamic Circle of North America (ICNA) Relief helps by offering humanitarian aid and combating poverty. Finally, **Mercy-USA for Aid and Development** is concerned with health and development around the world.

Islamic charities have sometimes become controversial because of apprehension that they are contributing to terrorist causes. The US Treasury Department has a list of banned organizations that are suspected of terrorism. It is advisable to check out each organization very carefully, especially since some of the suspect groups have taken names similar to recognized charities. For example, a US appeals court in 2011 reinstated the 2008 conviction of three men connected to Care international in Boston, a now defunct charity designed to help war orphans, widows, and refugees in Moslem countries, which was accused of unlawfully obtaining tax-exempt status for a jihadist organization. Their group is not connected with the global relief organization CARE international.[3]

A contrasting situation is provided by **Eboo Patel**, an Ismaili Moslem who is running a nonprofit organization called **The Interfaith Youth Core** to foster religious tolerance on college campuses. Instead of letting young Moslems and others be recruited by extremist groups, he is bringing together college students from diverse backgrounds to share in feeding the hungry, tutoring children, building houses, and other practical activities. He started the Youth Core in 2002 with a Jewish friend, a $35,000-Ford Foundation grant, decade, the Youth Core has been working on more than two hundred college and university campuses and on five continents to train thousands in interfaith leadership. They have run programs in church basements and White House conference rooms (www.ifyc.org).[4]

HINDU AND BUDDHIST CHARITIES

The Hindu and Buddhist world religious emphasize caring for others and contributing to a whole network of charities. Here is a brief list of some of these groups, which can be examined in greater detail by those wishing to contribute through their faiths.

A leading Hindu charity is **Hindu American Seva Charities** (HASC), dedicated to community service, education, grassroots social change, and build healthy societies (www.hinduamericanseva.org). Among others listed at the "heart of Hinduism: caring for others" are **Food for life** (ISKCON), **BAPS** (Swami Narayan Mission), **Ramakrishna Mission**, and **Friends of Vrindavana** (www.hinduism.iskcon.org).

Buddhism, another great world religion, has many organizations assisting their worshippers and others in the US and abroad. Among the charities listed by *Tricycle: The Buddhist Review* are: **Buddhist Global Relief, Himalayan Art Resources, Lotus Outreach, Nonviolent Peaceforce,** the **Karuna Center for Peacebuilding,** and **Foundation for the People of Burma** (www.tricycle.com).

Most, if not all, religions teach the importance of giving to others. Many people find it easiest, accordingly, to go first to their place of worship or organizations from their religious group to give charity to the less fortunate, provide educational facilities and programs, and provide a wide range of the other services.

JEWISH PHILANTHROPY

The great variety of Jewish religious, communal, and cultural bodies offers an example of how people nominally in the same religious group can have many approaches to philanthropy or "tzedaka" ("charity," derived from the Hebrew word for justice). The website www.tzedaka.org lists more than one hundred of the larger organizations but lacks room to delineate the may group chapters and smaller organizations.

Among the ways to analyze what is actually going on is to begin with the several religious denominations: Orthodox, Conservative, Reform, and Reconstructionist, each with its own religious institution and leadership. The outstanding educational institutions include **Yeshiva University** (Orthodox) led by **President Richard M. Joel,** the **Jewish Theological Seminary** (Conservative) headed by **Chancellor Arnold M. Eisen,** and the **Hebrew Union College-Jewish Institute of Religion** (Reform) led by **President Rabbi**

David Ellenson. In addition, there are many secular groups. All of the institutions have philanthropic and volunteer opportunities.

Then there are umbrella organizations that try to bring people together across their divisions, such as the **Jewish Community Relations Council (JCRC)** in New York and similar groups in other regions, to facilitate their ability to give and receive social services and to interact with other religious organizations.

The leading institution for Jewish philanthropy is the **Jewish Federations of North America,** which brings together local and regional federations. **UJA-Federation of NY,** the largest of these groupings, supports about one hundred local agencies educational and social services as well as building Jewish identify in New York and strengthening international Jewish communities' connections to each other and Jewish traditions. In addition to supporting Jews of all backgrounds, they also support New Yorkers of all ethnic origins. In New York, both because they receive some government funding and because Jewish values teach them to care for the stranger and all in need, they provide services to needy people regardless of religion, ethnicity, etc.[5]

In addition, there are many family foundations that choose the issues and methods they prefer to concentrate on. Many of them have come together in the **Jewish Funders Network**.

Several national and international organizations, such as the **American Jewish Committee, B'nai B'rith**, and the **Anti-Defamation League,** bring people together for social. Cultural. Philanthropic, and advocacy issues, at national and local levels. Many of the organizations are linked through the **World Jewish Congress** with Jewish communities in other countries.

Most of the organizations support the State of Israel, which was created in 1948 after the destruction of six million Jews in the Holocaust and have educational and social welfare programs in Israel. A notable example is **Hadassah** the women's Zionist organization. Many other organizations sponsor groups for educational, medical, environmental, and a wide range of other services.

Since higher education is so important for preparing people for serious careers and for research in science and the humanities, etc., **American Friends** groups provide support for **the Hebrew University of Jerusalem, the Technion Israel Institute of Technology, the Weizmann Institute, Tel Aviv University,** and many other universities and educational institutions.

The quest to preserve Jewish history and culture is such a central value that **Jewish museums** have been established in New York, Chicago, San Francisco, Los Angeles, Washington, D.C., Philadelphia, and elsewhere, supported by individual and community contributions.

Another special category of museums is devoted to preserving the memory of European Jewish life in the nineteenth and twentieth centuries and during the Holocaust through the **U.S. Holocaust Memorial Museum in Washington, D.C.** (sponsored mainly by the federal government), the **Museum of Jewish Heritages- A Living Memorial to the Holocaust in New York, the Museum of Tolerance of the Simon Wiesenthal Center in Los Angeles,** and many other smaller museums. Many individuals have made great contributions to preserving artifacts and educational programs. For example, **Fred Schwartz** used his business and organizational skills in his determination to found the **Auschwitz Jewish Center** to educate people about the Holocaust and genocide generally. During the time he was going back and forth from the US to Auschwitz to make his passion a reality, he was also fighting cancer. He told me he would not let himself be distracted by his health situation. Rather, he persevered so that the center could become an educational institution for the American service academies, as well as for university students and other visitors. The center united with the NY Museum of Jewish Heritage in 2006.[6]

Preserving records of American Jewish history is also a central concern and is carried out ably by the **American Jewish Archives of the Hebrew Union College-Jewish Institute of Religion** in Cincinnati (www.americanjewisharchives.org). the **American Jewish Historical Society** (www.ajhs.org), which is part of the **Center for Jewish History** (www.cjh.org) in New York, and other institutions.

Jewish education and communal service are important while students are on college campuses and beyond. The central organization serving them is the **Hillel Foundation,** with headquarters in the US and abroad. Among their affiliates are the **AEPi fraternity** chapters on many campuses, which emphasize philanthropy. The students and alumni are influential in choosing which charities they want to support.

On the local level in the US, each Jewish denomination has its own synagogues and all of them emphasize "tzedaka" or charity (parallel to efforts in local churches, mosques, and other religious canter).

For anyone who wants to give to others, it is clear that religious philanthropy offers a wide spectrum of opportunities. It just takes searching out the right institutions for you and the kind of activities (local, regional, national, international) where you feel you can make your greatest contributions.

* * *

B. IMPROVING K-12 EDUCATION (KINDERGARTEN THROUGH HIGH SCHOOL)

There is nothing more essential than providing a basic education to young people from pre-school and kindergarten through grade twelve. Yet the ongoing debates about teacher's competence, student test scores, and public versus chapter schools indicate widely divergent views and enormous criticism of what is going on in elementary education. Since the needs and the challenges are so great, there is room for different approaches by government, foundations, and individuals.

The major debate, according to **Joel Klein,**[1] reviewing *Class Warfare* by **Steven Brill**, is between "traditionalists" on the one side, represented mainly y teachers' unions arguing that to get people out of poverty, we must increase teacher's salaries and funds for public education. On the other side are reformers, who emphasize offering incentives to better teachers and principals, and alternative, chapter schools.

Fortunately, many private individuals and foundations are contributing in substantial ways to improve K-12 education. Let me give some examples of dedicated people who want to reform and improve education, especially for disadvantaged youth.

The outstanding example is **TEACH FOR AMERICA,** started in 1990 by **Wendy Kopp** based on proposal she made in her Princeton 1989 undergraduate senior thesis. The goal is to enlist top students from major colleges to teach all over the country, especially in regions with the neediest schools. By 2011, there were already about seventeen thousand Teach for America alumni.

Approximately seventy-three hundred corps members taught more than four hundred and fifty thousand students in the 2009-2010 school year. Many alumni have continued in teaching careers, often as principals, while others have used their experience in other professions. Ms. Kopp looks on Teach for America as a social movement to improve education for the poor. "We have the potential to end educational inequity, "she said. "I truly believe that."[2]

Richard Barth, who originally assisted Ms. Kopp and is now her husband, went on in 2005 to run the Knowledge Is Power Program, or **KIPP**, a charter school network that improves education, especially for low-income students. KIPP was founded by two Teach for America alumni, **Dave Levin and Michael Feinberg**, in Houston and the Bronx. It has grown to a national network of around one hundred schools. Mr. Barth said, "In a country as great as ours, why should where you're born dictate your life outcome... Anyone, born anywhere, should have access to high quality schools.[3] Among the earliest supporters for both Teach for American and KIPP, from 2000, were **Doris and Donald Fisher,** founders of the Gap clothing chain.

Since Bill Gates is concerned with the danger that deteriorating schools will lead to a small, educated underclass, the **Bill and Melinda Gates Foundation** has given around $5 billion to education grants and scholarships from 2000 to 2001 and has been supporting charter schools, especially in inner-city neighborhoods. KIPP has been a major recipient. The Gates Foundation is also sponsoring studies to evaluate teacher effectiveness and many other programs.

The **Walton Family Foundation,** the second biggest private funder after the Gates Foundation, is concentrating its education improvement grants on new schools, upgrading existing facilities, education policy, Teach for American, and charter schools.

Mark Zuckerberg, who co-founded the social network Facebook, pledged $100 million in 2010 to establish his foundation, Startup: Education. He had been inspired by the experiences of his wife, Priscilla Chan, as a teacher working in public schools through Teach for America. Zuckerberg was attracted to **Cory Booker,** Newark's mayor, whom he met at a conference, and decided to back his plans for improving Newark's school system.[4]

Dedication to teaching can carry beyond an individual classroom. For example, **Valerie Rowe,** a former teacher, gave $1 million to **Student Sponsor Partners,** which grants scholarships to at-risk high school students at twenty-six schools, mostly Catholic ones, around New York. Each student receives a mentor to guide him or her through four years of high school. About fourteen hundred were part of the program in 2011, its twenty-fifth year. Mrs. Rowe began as an elementary school teacher before earning a doctorate at Fordham University and then becoming a professor of education there. Her mother and daughters have been teachers. In addition, her husband, John W. Rowe, is a physician and a faculty member of Columbia University's School of Public Health after having been chair and CEO of Aetna Inc. He received scholarship throughout high school, college, and medical school and now wants to help others.[5]

Let's say you want to make a difference, but you can't become a teacher. You can contribute through **DonorsChoose.org** to your choice of classrooms. Public school teachers from all over the US post requests for what they need most: microscope slides for a biology class or musical instruments for a school recital. You can look through the projects. When the funding goals for particular projects are reached, Donors Choose will deliver the requested materials to the schools. You will get photos of your project being carried out, along with the teacher's thank-you letter and a report showing how the funds were spent. If you give over one hundred dollars, you will also get hand-written thank you notes from the students. They call this "citizen philanthropy," where everyone can receive the choice, transparency, and feedback usually reserved for mega contributions. DonorsChoose.org was founded by **Charles best** in 2000 when he was a social studies teacher at a Bronx high school in response to lack of educational materials at his school. He felt many people would want to help needy public-school classrooms if they some say over where their contributions were going. They could choose local schools or those in other places they were concerned about and could help in many fields.

For some educators, the goal is to provide the tools for faculty and students to use the latest technology to do significant research and teaching. For example, **Dr. Charlotte K. Frank**, who is senior vice president of research and development at McGraw-Hill Education, has established the Dr. Charlotte K. Frank Center for Mathematics Education at the City College of New York, where she received her bachelor's in business administration degree, majoring in math and minoring on statistics. In addition, she gave a substantial gift to Hunter College, where she received her Ms. Ed., to create a new model classroom with the latest technology for teaching in P-12 school.[6] She also gave another major gift to NYU, where she received her Ph. D., to establish a Science/STEM (Science, Technology, Engineering, and Mathematics) Center. In addition, she donated the Frank Family Virtual Planetarium and telescope facility at the Arad High School for Aviation and Aerospace in Israel. After receiving more than sixty awards for her work, Dr. Frank was inducted into the Association of Education Publishers 2011 Hall of Fame (www.aepweb.org).

Principals count, too, in improving schools. The **Wallace Foundation** is committing $75 million over five years to training and supporting principals in six school districts in North Carolina, Georgia, Florida, and Maryland, as well as Detroit and New York City. The districts were chosen because they already have rigorous programs for training principals.[7]

Individuals continue to reach out to help poorer families, many of them because they grew up poor and, through education, were able to advance themselves. **Steven B. Klinsky,** who benefited from daily tutoring by his older brother, determined to help early childhood education after his brother died. He searched for a school where the need was greatest and decided on a poor school in Brooklyn, where a teacher could train children in reading, math, and language skills in groups of twenty. The original group was replicated in four other Brooklyn schools, so by 2011, about one thousand students were being helped.[8]

Another advocacy effort for children is the **Citizens' Committee for Children in New York,** which is being assisted by **Ricki Tigert Helfer and Michael Helfer.** They became involved after Ms. Helfer took their multi-week community leadership course, which brings volunteers to learn more about children's issues, including poverty, juvenile detention, and health care, through their playing the roles of parents who face many challenges when they are attempting to get services for their children.[9]

A program to use yoga to enhance learning in the classroom is aimed at students in disadvantaged schools to help the young people be more attentive, energized and focused in school. The **Rachel Greene Memorial Fund** at **Zina Greene** in memory of her daughter, who was a yoga teacher, awards scholarships and stipends to yoga, classroom, and gym teachers for training to bring yoga into disadvantaged schools. With the help of additional sponsors, teachers trained by the fund's scholarships and stipends have, since 2006, spread throughout the country, from Appalachia to Dade Country to Boston.[10]

To help visually impaired preschool children. **Ethel Lefrak** is giving $2 million to **Lighthouse International,** a leading charity for assisting blind people, to provide technology to help upgrade their program.[11]

What happens to people who have had to drop out of school? One way to bring them back into advancement opportunities is to enable them to get high school equivalency diplomas (GEDs). **Margaret Grace** has been an inspiring leader for reaching out to low-income women of all ages in the **Grace Outreach Group** established in 2004 in the South Bronx (www.graceoutreachbronx.org). The co-chair of the group, **Kelly Millet,** has given more than $100,000 to them to help women complete their GED qualifications out of gratitude for the way his parents encouraged him to complete his education. In the program's first seven years, it enabled about seven hundred women to receive their diplomas. Some of them have returned to the program as tutors and mentors to prepare the next group of women to attain their GEDs.[12]

Some donors believe in the benefits of music and art education for less advantaged students. For example, **Edmund Schroeder** co-founded **Education Through Music,** which supports music classes at elementary and middle schools that would not be able to offer them otherwise. By 2011, the organization was serving nineteen thousand school children in New York, San Francisco, and Los Angeles. They have also provided consulting services to school districts in New Haven, Philadelphia, and St. Louis.[13]

Since 2004, the **Harmony Program at the City University of New York** has been training college music students to teach disadvantaged elementary school students to play instruments in daily after-school music lessons. One of the major supporters is **Roy Niederhoffer,** who feels that the training helps the students learn skills and develop discipline. The program also provides approximately one hundred students with instruments, books, and the chance to attend cultural events.[14]

Lin Arison gave about $39 million to endow the **National Foundation for Advancement in the Arts** in Miami, which she and her late husband, **Ted Arison,** founded in 1981 to help young artists in their careers. Proceeds from the new endowment will support new arts education programs for high school students and teachers at a time of tightened budgets.[15]

LeRoy Neiman, a well-known artist, has given $1 million to Arts Horizons, a non-profit organization for education in art music, dance, and theater in the New York area, to found the **LeRoy Neiman Art Center** in central Harlem. The goal is to have professionals teach low-cost classes for people of all ages.[16]

Another innovative approach for education comes from **Angelica Berrie** of Teaneck, New Jersey, who has given money to an organization in Israel to retrofit buses with computers and modern technology, including robots, to become mobile classrooms. There are now eight such buses going to sixty communities.

So much has been done and so much more needs to be done to enhance education from pre-kindergarten through high school. Your contributions can be meaningful at whatever level you choose: local, national, or international.

* * *

C. HIGHER EDUCATION

Universities and colleges are essential for educating students from a diversity of backgrounds and for furthering research in the humanities and social sciences, biological and physical sciences, and other areas that make our civilization. Leading donors have furthered advances in both widening opportunities for students and enhancing basic and applied research.

University presidents can make a great difference by providing comprehensive plans to enhance facilities and increase opportunities for growth of individuals and society. An outstanding example is **Columbia University,** where **Lee C. Bollinger** took the helm in 2002 after establishing himself as a leading legal scholar of the First Amendment, freedom of speech, and affirmative action in university admissions. He had served as Law School dean and then president of the University of Michigan. As Columbia president, he has been leading a major expansion effort in intellectual activities, physical space, international connections, and student aid. He and his associates have mobilized alumni and others to enhance the university.

The foremost donor of scholarships has been **John Kluge,** who gave $510 million to Columbia University for scholarships. He came to the US at eight form Germany, grew up in Detroit, and benefited from a Columbia scholarship during the Depression. As with many others who want to give back, he said, "If it hadn't been for Columbia, my path would have been entirely different in life. Columbia gave me an opportunity, and the only way you can really repay that opportunity is for you to help someone else," [1]

Among the top intellectual expansion efforts has been the donation of $250 million by Dawn Greene and the Jerome L. Greene Foundation to establish the **Jerome L. Greene Science Center** in 2006. It will be home to the Mind, Brain and Behavior Initiative. The donation will add to the existing strengths in neurological research by top scientists in the field and create new opportunities for exploration of the brain in the sciences and the arts and to develop new cures for diseases.

In addition, **H.F. "Gerry" Lenfest** pledged $30 million in 2011 for the Lenfest Center for the Arts on Columbia's new "Manhattanville" campus. He and his wife, Marguerite, will have given more than $100 million for many programs, including the endowment of thirty-two new professorships, a law school residence hall, the Lenfest Center for Sustainable Energy at Columbia's Earth Institute, and awards for outstanding teaching. Mr. Lenfest, who is a Columbia trustee, said he doesn't believe "in dying with a lot of wealth."[2]

Loyalty and generosity to Columbia are also exemplified by **Laurans Mendelson,** who graduated both from Columbia College and its Graduates School of Business. Mr. Mendelson's father. Samuel received his A.B from Columbia in 1906. Both of his sons, Eric and Victor, received their bachelor's degree from Columbia College, while Eric also went on to an M.B.A. from the business school. Now that there are six children in the fourth generation, they will probably also study at Columbia. Meanwhile, Mr. Mendelson, who was a Columbia trustee and is my cousin, established The Laurans and Arlene Mendelson Professorship Chair in Economics at the college and the business school, the Mendelson Professorship Chair in American Studies at the college, and in honor of his parents, the Samuel and Blanche Mendelson Scholarship Fund at Columbia College.

A successful business leader and head of many nonprofit organizations, **John Whitehead**, who was co-chairman of Goldman Sachs from 1976 to 1984, felt the importance of management training for people working for nonprofits. For this reason, he gave $10 million to the **Harvard Business School** in 1995 to establish the **John C. Whitehead fund for Not-for-Profit Management.** While he was planning his gift, he learned that he and other major businessmen had lent their names to a charity called New Era for Philanthropy, which turned out to be a Ponzi scheme. This made him even more determined to bring business management skills to non-profits.[3]

Another major contribution to enhancing education at **Harvard University** is the gift by **Rita and Gustave Hauser** of $40 million in 2011 to launch the Harvard Initiative for Learning and Teaching. This adds to their previous gifts of the **Houser Center for Nonprofit Organizations** at the Kennedy School, a building for the Harvard

Law School, and the Rita E. Houser professorship of human rights and humanitarian law.

American values put a great emphasis on education and on rising in society through one's own efforts. An outstanding example of a self-made man who has been determined to create opportunities for others is **Lawrence N. Field,** who went from a poor home in the East Bronx to found a successful real estate empire in New York and Southern California. To enable others to follow his path, he gave $10 million to establish the **Lawrence N. Field Center for Entrepreneurship** at his alma mater, **Baruch College in New York**, in 1998. He was building on a small business lab originally funded in 1993 by the City University of New York and Baruch College **Zicklin School of Business** (named for another successful alumnus donor). The center offers courses on entrepreneurship to at least six hundred fulltime students plus many more part-time students. It also provides counsel and assistance to many small businesses. They bring together educators, government, and the private sector. Mr. Field said, "Like many young people in our country today, I was the son of poor immigrants who struggled to give me an education. I am an example of what can be achieved in America regardless of your origins, and I want to help the next generation of entrepreneurs understand that they too are limited only by their ambition and hardwork."[4]

The first African-American **Yale** graduate to become a major donor is **William H. Wright II,** who gave $1 million to Yale in 2007 to establish the Wright Reading Room in the library. Wright, who was a Morgan Stanley managing director, also served on many boards, including those of Donors Choose, the NYC Ballet, and various hospitals. Since he graduated from Yale in 1982, he was also one of the youngest major donors to the university.[5]

The popularity of giving scholarships to alma mater or other higher education institutions is evident in the list of the fifty biggest givers in 2010, as recorded in *The Chronicle of Philanthropy*, "Philanthropy 50." Some examples, in alphabetical order, include **Mary E. McKinney,** who left at least $25 million to the **University of Texas at San Antonio** for scholarships. **Edward H. and Vivian Merrin** gave $30.2 million to **Tufts University** to establish a new scholarship fund, especially because it was a recession year. Another couple who emphasized scholarships was **Howard G. and Louise Phanstiel,** who gave $20.02 million to **Syracuse University** for middle-income students who are US citizens. **Paul and Daisy M. Soros,** who came to the US from Hungary in 1948 with scarce resources, but then prospered together with Paul's brother, George, donated $25 million to establish the **Paul & Daisy Soros Fellowship for New Americans** for graduate studies in any subject in any US university. Another refugee couple, **Jan T. and Marica F. Vilcek**, who came to the US from then Communist Czechoslovakia, gave the **NYU Langone Medical Center** $23.1 million or scholarships, as well as a new residence hall for students.

FURTHERING RESEARCH

The goal of every research institution is to increase knowledge and understanding of major issues in the humanities and sciences. The opportunities are vast, as anyone who has sat on university boards (as I have) can attest. At the same time, each institution has to set priorities depending on its major areas of expertise and the willingness of donors to fund central explorations.

Eli and Edythe Broad gave $400 million for genetics research to the Broad Institute of MIT and Harvard in 2008. The institute endeavors to find genetic links among major diseases and to discover the molecular causes of disease with the goal of diagnosing and preventing illnesses and developing medicines. Another positive feature is encouraging collaboration among scientists from other institutions around the world and interaction among mathematicians, engineers, physicists, and scientists from other disciplines.

It is encouraging when scientists who have developed practical applications for their work and prospered thereby contribute to further scientific research. Such is the case with **Charles Simonyi and James H. Simons,** two mathematicians who contributed a combined $100 million in 2011 to the Princeton Institute for Advanced Study.

On the humanities side, **NYU** benefited from a $200 million gift in 2006 from the **Leon Levy Foundation** to create the Institute for the

Study of the Ancient World. The Institute is expanding opportunities for both research and teaching about Greece, Rome, the Middle East, and other ancient civilizations. This covers the history, archaeology, literature, art, etc. of antiquity (www.leonlevyfoundation.org).6

SPONSORING LECTURES, CONFERENCES, SEMINARS, PUBLICATION: GIFTS WITH MORE MODEST RESOURSES

A great way to stimulate discussion of major new ideas and to disseminate knowledge on important issues is to sponsor a lecture, conference, publication, etc. with a university, institution, or organization with which you are already affiliated or one you admire and wish to become a more active participant in. You can also give your collections of books, digital materials, art etc. to your favorite institutions.

LECTURES

Talks can be one-time, annual, periodic, or whatever other format you and the institution find suitable. They can take place over one year or more, or a decade or two, and then eventually may be endowed. You or the institution's staff can invite the most knowledgeable, well-known, and stimulating speakers. There is one potential drawback: if the weather is inclement or some crisis intervenes, the attending audience may be less than expected. How effective, then, is the effort? Your program can still have an impact even without a maximum audience:

1) The publicity before the event will bring the speaker, topic, and your sponsorship to a wide audience that will become more aware of all three.
2) Many institutions tape the programs and video stream them directly to a worldwide audience both simultaneously with the actual program or available on their website in video, audio, and/or transcripts.
3) Publishing the texts of the lectures, etc. as reprints. A small pamphlet can be circulated by mail or e-mail through the

organizing institution. On the other hand, since one piece can easily be lost or overlooked, it is often better to publish it also in a recognized journal or a cohesive series of stand-alone publications.
4)   The Internet offers many opportunities to circulate texts to a larger audience.

CONFERENCES AND SEMINARS

One of the best ways to bring knowledgeable people from diverse fields together to deal with major issues is to hold a special conference on the topic, which can transcend and cross-fertilize existing specialty boundaries.

While it may run into six figures to sponsors a major conference, the innovative donor can contribute **SEED MONEY** so that the conference organizers can start deciding on the theme, venue, major desired speakers, etc. Then the organizers will be in a strong position when they approach major foundations and other donors for funding.

Another desirable format is to hold a weekly, monthly, or annual seminar on a major subject. If the innovative donor will give a certain basic sum to cover the cost of administration, possibly room rental, discussion materials. Etc., the participants will pay for attending and refreshments.

RESULTS

How can you tell whether your programs are having an impact?

1)   If your seed money leads to a conference that then sparks debate in a larger framework over a number of years. Alternatively, if other conferences and organizations take up similar themes and broaden the discussion
2)   If the lecture or program you sponsor leads to publication in print or on the web and possibly to a book, all or which may be cited by other authors and stimulate further discussions and publications.

60

GIVING COLLECTIONS OF BOOKS, MEDIA, ARTWORK, ETC.

If you have a particular expertise or have spent years collecting materials in certain specialized fields, your collections can be valuable to universities, libraries, or other institutions. It is important to research the existing holdings of the intended institution to ascertain if your materials make sense for them. Then a lot will depend on finding the proper authorities with whom to negotiate your gift. Some people are more imaginative and flexible about accepting new sources.

MY EXPERIENCE SPONSORING LECTURES, CONFERENCES, SEMINARS, PUBLICATIONS, BOOK AND ARTS COLLECTIONS, AND MORE

A graphic example of how giving is not just for the very rich is the range of conferences, seminars, public forums, publications, book and art collections, scholarships, and more I have been sponsoring for over thirty years at Columbia University, the Hebrew University of Jerusalem, the City University Graduate Center, NYU, and other educational institutions. I have been originating ideas and then implementing them through consultation and hands-on participation with the appropriate people for each program. The process has created great élan in my life and benefited many people. By presenting some of the highlights in detail, I can show you how complicated the negotiations can be among various scholars and departments within one university, let alone among several institutions. With persistence, programs can evolve and reach many people as part of our efforts to analyze and improve societies.

The first step is to find the most capable scholars and administrators who are truly dedicated to research, teaching, and to advancing international and domestic policies and development. The second is to find crucial and innovative areas in which to invest our efforts.

Through the years, I have brought or received ideas in discussions with people I respect at Columbia and other institutions of higher learning and evolved feasible programs with them. Thus, as I have no children of my own, the many programs that emerged have become like my "children."

Since I have wished to be innovative and influential in the educational process, I established the **Dr. Susan Aurelia Gitelson Fund for Innovative Programs** at the **Columbia School of International and Public Affairs (SIPA)** in 1998. The led to my sponsoring the **Gitelson Symposium on "Public Service in the Private Sector"** in 2001, which encouraged idealistic alumni to take jobs in finance, international business, etc., while at the same time contributing time and money to charitable causes. Subsequently, I sponsored the **Gitelson Policy Forum** in 2005-2009 to bring outstanding Columbia scholars on major international issues to SIPA alumni gatherings at the Columbia University Club in midtown New York. The programs were also videotaped to be broadcast to alumni and others all over the world.

Meanwhile, to broaden educational possibilities, I began the **Dr. Susan Aurelia Gitelson Fund for Innovation Programs** at the **Columbia Faculty of Arts and Sciences** in 2000. In conjunction with the **Institute for Social and Economic Policy (ISERP)** and particularly **Professor David Stark's Center on Organizational Innovation (COI),** I first sponsored a very lively roundtable on "New Spaces for Civil Society in Latin America and Eastern Europe: Strengthening or Fragmenting Democracy?" in 2001. Which was apparently the first multidisciplinary, comparative interchange on these subjects by a wide range of regional and disciplinary experts at the university.

In response to the September 11, 2001 ("9/11") terrorist attacks on the World Trade Center in New York, I gave seed money for the first comprehensive conference held to consider how to rebuild downtown New York in the aftermath of the destruction. The gathering called **"EVOLVE NEW YORK Open Studio: Rebuilding Proposals"** was held on May 9-10, 2002, and included the widest range of scholars probably ever assembled for such an undertaking, including mainly ISERP, COI, and the Urban Planning Program of the Columbia Graduate School of Architecture and Planning. Other participants included businesspeople, financiers, and designers. For the first time. Local organizations were invited to give their views on making the space more attractive for neighborhood people (www. coi.columbia.edu). At the **City University Graduate Center of New York's Ralph Bunche Institute on the United Nations,** I sponsored the **Moses Leo Gitelson Seminar on the UN,** 1981-2002. First under **Ambassador Seymour Maxwell Finger** and the under **Prof. Benjamin Rivlin**, we hosted top figures from diplomatic missions, UN administrations, academic researchers, and many more in weekly luncheon sessions.

One of my greatest concerns has always been to promote peace in the Middle East and around the world, especially by facilitating cooperative research possibilities at institutions of higher learning, particularly at the **Harry S. Truman Research Institute on the Advancement of Peace at the Hebrew University of Jerusalem** through the **American Friends of the Hebrew University (AFHU).** With this in mind. I sponsored two editions of **"PATHS TO PEACE: Research Cooperation Across Borders in the Middle East"** at the Truman Institute in 1999 and 2006. When my Gitelson Peace Prize was transformed into the Truman Peace Prize (see "Awards" chapter), I decided as an alternative to sponsor a series of special **Gitelson Peace Papers** at the Truman Institute beginning in 1993 dealing with the Middle East, Africa, Asia, and Latin America, as well as the US and Europe. The papers have been like ambassadors to facilitate scholars and institutions.

Another area where I have followed my father's example is to give book and art collections to university libraries. Thus, I gave my rare books collections to the New York University Fales Rare Book Library and various other collections to Columbia University, Rutgers University, Queens College, Brenau University in Gainesville, Georgia, and the Hebrew University of Jerusalem.

These examples of contributions to higher education by university administrators, scholars, and donors illustrate how much has been done to enable students of limited means to attend suitable schools and to advance knowledge in many significant areas. Of course, with imagination and a willingness to devote assets of time, money, contacts, and other resources, the future possibilities for expanding higher education can be limitless.

* * *

D. SCIENCE AND HEALTH

Many people contribute to cure and eventually to eliminate heart disease, cancer, and other maladies both through scientific research and medical and hospital care. The first place to turn to Combat a specific disease is a major organization that supports research for the causes of the disease and ways to find a cure, as well as providing the most advanced care possible. The **American Heart Association, Inc.,** for example, targets two of the major killers: cardiovascular disease and stroke. Since its founding in 1924, it has become the nation's oldest and largest voluntary organization fighting heart disease and stroke though research, public and professional educational programs, and public health advocacy campaigns (www. heart.org and www2.guidestar.org).

The **American Cancer Society**, which is the largest voluntary health organization in the US, administers programs with hospitals, research centers, ad medical and lay volunteers. It runs programs nationally, as well as through its twelve divisions and in local communities. There are more than three million dedicated volunteers at all levels engaged in a multi-pronged approach: prevention, research to find cures, and action campaigns to fight back (e.g., anti-smoking campaigns). They organize around five thousand relays for life, plus marches, marathons, cycling, and other endurance events around the US. They also sponsor a movement for more birthdays in their efforts to prolong life (www.cancer.org).

DEVOTION TO ELIMINATING A DISEASE OR CURING PEOPLE WHO SUFFER FROM IT BECAUSE YOU OR YOUR LOVED ONES HAVE HAD IT

In addition to the major organizations fighting diseases, there are also campaigns and contributions made by people who have suffered from a particular disease or who have lost a loved one through a malady like cancer. A prime example of this is the **Susan G. Komen for the Cure Foundation**, which was started by **Nancy G. Brinker** in memory of her sister who had died of breast cancer. Komen for the Cure is the global leaders in the breast cancer movement. From its inception in 1982 through 2011, it has invested more than $1.9 billion in breast cancer research and programs (www.komen.org). It is a striking example of how using business techniques can considerably increase the funds raised.[1]

Evelyn H. Lauder, who married into the famous cosmetics firm started by her mother-in-law, Estee Lauder, found out she had breast cancer in 1989. Her reaction was to advocate measures to improve women's health and to found the **Breast Cancer Research Foundation** in 1993. By the time she died in 2011 from ovarian cancer, the foundation had raised more than $350 million.[2] It had also been cooperating with Komen for the Cure.

After his father and two sisters had died of cancer, **Robert A. Belfer** and his wife, **Renee**, have $100 million to the Weill Cornell Medical College to establish the **Belfer Medical Research Building**. The center, which is expected to open in 2014, will focus on a number of urgent health issues, including cancer, cardiovascular disease, and age-related conditions like Alzheimer's. The gift continues a long-time relationship with the college, including saving Bob Belfer's life when he was twenty-four years old. "Here is this mega-research project in an institution that is so close and meaningful to us," he said, "so it's an opportunity of a lifetime."[3]

Eva Andersson-Dubin is both a physician and a cancer survivor who wants to coordinate the best kind of cancer care for others. To this end, she and her husband, **Glenn Dubin**, have donated $15 million and raised ore funds for the **Dubin Breast Cancer** at the Mount Sinai Medical Center in New York City.[4]

The loss of his eleven-year old son to brain cancer led **Stephen J. Czech** to establish the **Mikey Czech Foundation** to fund pediatric brain-tumor research at the Dana Farber Cancer Institute, Harvard Medical School, and the Broad Institute in Boston.[5]

The **Monti family** at Long Island contributes care, research, and education, directed mainly to combat acute myeloid leukemia. **Caroline Monti Saladino** is president of the **Don Monti Memorial Research Foundation**, named for her brother who died of myeloblastic leukemia in 1972. Since then, she, her parents, and other family members have been contributing time and money to support research to find a cure at Cold Spring Harbor Laboratory, while also helping patient care and a bone-marrow transplant program at North Shore University Hospital in Manhasset and other hospitals in the region.[6]

Lawrence Golub and his wife, **Karen Finerman**, who are both involved in finance, have given $500,000 to the **New York Stem Cell Foundation** to establish the **Golub Stem Cell Initiative for Parkinson's Disease** since several close relatives have the disease. According to Mr. Golub, the donation is going "where it can have very leverage output."[7]

Obie Harrington-Howes, who had coached hundreds of children in Connecticut's hockey and lacrosse leagues, suffered a spinal-cord injury while swimming. This inspired him to establish a foundation in 1999 to help people with spinal injuries. The foundation had given about $2 million by 2011 to more than two hundred people for their rehabilitation.[8]

ADDITIONAL CONTRIBUTORS TO SCIENTIFIC RESEARCH AND MEDICAL CARE

Some insight into the backgrounds, motivations, and choices of individuals and families who have contributed to scientific research and medical care can be found in a group of the "Philanthropy 50" donors for 2010 in *The Chronicle of Philanthropy*, February 4,2011 (www.philanthropy.com).

Charles E. Kaufman, who was a purchasing director at Merck and an investor, made a lot of money later in his life, which enabled him to leave $53.3 million to the Pittsburgh Foundation. The majority of the gift will fund the **Charles E. Kaufman Foundation** he started in 2005 for research in biology, chemistry, and physics. It gives awards "for achievement in and contribution to the field and to humanity." When he died at ninety-seven, few people knew he had made a fortune by investing in chemical engineering, the field he had studied. He hoped his research fund would enable a scientist to win a Nobel Prize. He explained when he gave one of his awards, "I can accomplish more through others that I ever could myself."[9]

A former chairman of Merck, **Dr. Roy Vagelos**, and his wife, **Diana**, gave $50 million to the **Columbia University Medical Center**. Since techniques taught in graduate and medical schools have changed a lot over time, they want their gift to offer students the most advanced tools as they are developed.

Although **Lee G. and Jane H. Seidman** had always responded to philanthropic request in various fields and different parts of the country, they finally decided to concentrate on one or two non-profits and no more than one or two geographic areas. Thus, they pledged $42 million in establish the **University Hospitals Seidman Cancer Center.** They had also pledged another $23 million to the Cleveland Clinic a few years earlier.

As Americans, we are proud that our countrymen help people in other parts to the world. Fortunately, the process can be reciprocal: we also benefit from the gifts of people who come to the US to study and live and then decide to give back to their adopted country. Coincidentally, for example, two Asian-Americans gave $50 million each for scientific research in 2010. **Ming Hsieh** came from China to the US when he was twenty-four and succeeded financially through several information technology companies he founded. At age fifty-five, he pledged $50 million to the University of Southern California (USC) to endow a new institute to use nanomedicine to combat cancer through new drugs and therapies. A Japanese-American,

Paul Ichiro Terasaki, who is a retired professor of surgery at the University of California at Los Angeles (UCLA) and an entrepreneur in human tissues for organ transplants, gave $50 million to UCLA in 2010, when he was eighty-two, for a life sciences building and to endow a surgery professorship. In 2006, he had already given UCLA $5 million for a program to augment better understanding between Japan and the US.

USC has also benefited from a combined $260 million donation from the **W. M. Keck Foundation.** This represents the biggest commitment for a medical institution from a private foundation west of the Mississippi. The resulting divisions included the Keck Hospital, Keck Doctors, and the Keck School of Medicine of USC.[10] The donor, **William Myron Keck**, came to Southern California from Pennsylvania and succeeded in oil exploration. He established the Superior Oil Company in 1921 and his own foundation in 1954.

Edward Taylor developed a lung cancer medication, Alimta, and then used his royalties to donate $16 million to his alma mater, Hamilton College, in upstate New York for their science center. He is now an emeritus professor at Princeton and runs the **SunUp Foundation** with his wife. Their gift will go for financial aid, science research, and art facilities.[11]

Since getting well depends a great deal on how doctors treat their patients, **Carolyn and Matthew Bucksbaum for Clinical Excellence** at the University of Chicago Medical Center. The director will be their physician **Dr. Mark Siegler,** who believes, "To care for a patient, you have to care about a patient. "The institute's main goal will be to improve how medical students handle the doctor-patient relationship.[12]

So much more remains to be done in basic and applied scientific research, as well as in treating diseases and improving health worldwide. Consequently, multiple giving opportunities will continue to exist for enhancing the quality of life for people everywhere.

* * *

E. ARTS, CULTURE, AND THE HUMANITIES

INDIVIDUAL DONORS TO ART MUSEUMS, OPERA, MUSIC, LITERATURE, AND THEATER

Whereas in Europe and many other parts of the world, the great museums and the other arts institutions are built and maintained by the state (e.g. the Louvre in Paris), most American museums and collections within institutions (such as the Metropolitan Museums of Art in New York. The Art Institute of Chicago, the Boston Museum of Fine Arts, and the Los Angeles Country Museum) originate from individual donors. The major exception is the Smithsonian Institution in Washington, D.C., which has a whole complex of museums, mostly national, but still has gifts from individuals, such as the Hirshhorn Museum, based on the collection of **Joseph Hirshhorn.**

Many of the great cultural institutions retain the names of their founding donors, as is particularly evident in New York. Among the many institutions based on great industrial and financial fortunes are a whole group of **Rockefeller family** benefactions from various family members given to the Museum of Modern Art, the Asia Society, the Michael C. Rockefeller Wing of the Metropolitan Museum, and many more. It addition are the cultural institutions endowed by **John Pierpont Morgan, Jr., Henry Frick,** and others. The Guggenheim Museum, which was founded by **Solomon R. Guggenheim** in New York, also operates a branch in Bilbao, Spain, the **Peggy Guggenheim** Collection in Venice, Italy, and other programs. The Whitney Museum of American Art was founded by **Gertrude Vanderbilt Whitney** based on her collection of American artists she knew from around the time she opened her museum in 1931 after the Metropolitan Museum had declined her offer to donate them. Ironically, the Metropolitan in 2011 bought the building used by the Whitney before its projected move downtown, probably to house part of its own contemporary art holdings.

Among the more recent museums opened in New York are the Neue Galerie dedicated to early twentieth-century German and Austrian art and design based on the collections of **Ronald S. Lauder** and **Serge Sabarsky**, which opened in 2001, In addition, the Rubin Museum of Art was established in 2004 by **Donald and Shelley Rubin** to display Himalaya art.

Since the museums and other cultural institutions always want to upgrade their facilities and to expand, the donor opportunities are enormous. One example is a gift to the Museum of the City of New York by **James Dinan**, its board chair, of $1 million in 2011 to finance the new core exhibit of New York's cultural, political, and economic history in extensive multimedia installations.

Myriad museums pat tribute to their donor's collections throughout the US, for example, the **Isabella Stewart Gardner** Museum founded in 1903 in Boston, Massachusetts, and the Menil Collection in Fort Worth, Texas, opened by **Dominique de Menil** in 1987. Los Angeles has the **J. Paul Getty** Museum and the **Board** Contemporary Art Museum, among many others.

The newest privately donated museum is in Bentonville, Arkansas. **Alice L. Walton** has collected major American artwork for her Crystal Bridges Museum of American Art opened in 2011. It is noteworthy because she wants to make his town of thirty-five thousand a major destination for American art in the first such institution built in fifty years. The Walton fortune dates back only to 1962, when her father, **Sam Walton,** founded his first Wal-Mart in Bentonville. Alice Walton has brought together six hundred paintings, and sculptures form the nineteenth and twentieth centuries with the help of consultants, but based mainly in her own studies in the field.[1]

While most of us are unlikely to found our own museums, we can still contribute artwork to major institutions or to local museums located throughout the US and abroad. We can also volunteer as docents and assist museums in many other ways. In addition, we can be mentors to bring disadvantaged children who have not grown up with the arts to visit museums, learn about the artists, and take classes. A dedicated member of a museum or other cultural institution can analyze existing programs and then create new ways to make the arts come alive for new generations. One can also establish art prizes to encourage and give prominence to hard-working contemporary artists.

The outstanding example of people of modest means collecting extensively and then offering their appreciated artwork to institutions all over the country is the **Dorothy and Herbert Vogel Collection: Fifty Works for Fifty States** (www.vogel5050.org). The Vogels befriended artists and gallery owners in New York and amassed an enormous collection of original contemporary American art, mainly Abstract Expressionists, Pop Art, etc., which they gave to the Library of Congress in 2008 for distribution all over the US. This then freed up space in their home for them to continue their collection.

All the arts can help enrich lives for people of all ages. For example, **Agnes Varis**, who came from a poor family but built a profitable generic drug company, contributed greatly to the Metropolitan Opera and other arts programs. Most notably, she and her husband started the Agnes Varis and **Karl Leichtman** Rush Tickets Programs in 2006 to make one-hundred-dollar orchestra seats available at twenty dollars during the week for seniors and others who might not otherwise be able to attend the opera.

One of the outstanding supporters of the arts is **James D. Wolfensohn**, former president of the World Bank, who was chairman of the board of Carnegie Hall in New York and the John F. Kennedy Center for the Performing Arts in Washington, D.C. He also chaired the Institute for Advanced Study in Princeton. **David M. Rubenstein,** another financier, has been chairman of the board of the Kennedy Center, and has been an active supporter of the National Archives, the Library of Congress, and the National Symphony Orchestra in Washington, D.C., Lincoln Center in New York, and other cultural and educational institutions.

The **Doris Duke Charitable Foundation** announced in 2011 that it would award $50 million during a ten-year period to over two hundred performing artists, dance companies, theaters, and presenters. The money may be allocated as flexible multi-year cash awards and will support residencies.[2]

New works by choreographers, musicians, playwrights, and others have been presented by top performers as part of the Works and Process series at the **Guggenheim Museum,** founded by **Mary Sharp Cronson** in the 1980s. The performances and discussions with the artists are followed by receptions, with opportunities for the audience members to interact with the performers.

The music director of the Los Angeles Philharmonic since 2010, **Gustavo Dudamel,** began as the music director of the Simon Bolivar Youth Orchestra in Venezuela. He has taken the Latin American model of El Sistema, which encourages hundreds of thousands of children each year to study musical instruments, to the US through Youth Orchestra of Los Angeles (YOLA), which also encourages less advantaged children to learn and develop through music.

The Pulitzer Prizes were established by the American publisher **Joseph Pulitzer** and have been administered by Columbia University. They award outstanding newspaper and online journalism, literature (including fiction, biography, and history), theater, and musical composition. Other prizes encouraging authors include the **Donald Windham Sandy M. Campbell** Literature Prizes, which will be awarded to playwrights and writers of fiction and nonfiction from 2013. The **Harold and Mimi Steinberg** Charitable Trust to advance American Theater has been supporting playwrights and nonprofits companies, including **Lincoln Center Theater.**

Opportunities abound for people to help opera, theater, music, summer stock, and other groups all over the country in cities and local communities. Many people can enjoy the creativity and esprit de corps of working together to produce works of art-not just as financial backers, but also as amateur costume and set designers, volunteer ticket sellers, usher, etc.

* * *

F. SPORTS

Since sports heroes are so important to Americans and people all over the world, it is important that many leading sports groups and individuals develop philanthropic programs. Meanwhile, people at national and local levels use walks and sport events to raise and contribute funds to eradicate diseases and other causes. A positive attitude toward helping others through sports begun at a young age or late can carry on throughout life.

TOP ATHLETES FROM BASEBALL, FOOTBALL, BASKETBALL, AND TENNIS SET EXAMPLE THROUGH WIDE-RANGING PROGRAMS

Here are some outstanding examples of sports heroes creating programs to help others. For instance, the **Major League Baseball Players Trust** since 1966 has been contributing to aid less fortunate people and inspiring others to follow their examples. Among the projects they have supported are partnering with **Volunteers of America** to supply affordable programs and services to thousands of young people and their families, such as daycare, safe playgrounds, and health care. They also teach baseball and life skills to less advantaged young people in inner cities across the US and conduct many programs to help areas devastated by natural disasters, such as hurricanes in the Gulf Region (www.mlbplayers.com).

Among the many baseball players who have launched their own programs, **Derek Jeter** of the New York Yankees stands out with his **Turn 2 Foundation** begun in 1996. The main goal is to enable young people to avoid drugs and alcohol and "turn 2" healthy lifestyles. This is done through centers, camping, and scholarships for thousands of young people (www.mlb.com).

Not to be outdone, the **National Football League** brought together many of football's biggest stars for the **Big Game Big Give at Super bowl XLV** in Indianapolis in 2012. Among the NFL's major new charitable efforts is the **NFL Super Bowl Celebrity Bowling Classic** in Dallas. It is a part of the **NFL Charities**, a non-profit group that has given more than $120 million to about six hundred and fifty organizations (www.halogentv.com).

A top football star, **Tom Brady** of the New England Patriots has been organizing the Tom Brady Football Challenge to benefits **Best Buddies International** since 2010.[1]

Justin Tuck, a Notre Dame and New York Giants football star, formed **R.U.S.H. for Literacy** to donate books to children in Alabama, where he grew up, and New York City. The initials stand for "read, understand, succeed, and hope" all ways that a man can inspire other young people to study and advance in the world. In 2011, at twenty-eight, he had already given more than twenty-one thousand books and raised $800,000.[2]

It is important, however, not to be so impressed with a sport celebrity that you and society forget to scrutinize his actions and what happens at a charity he has started. A major scandal finally broke out at Penn State in 2011 when a long-time football coach, **Jerry Sandusky,** was charged with forty counts of sexually abusing young boys in the **Second Mile charity** he had founded in 1977. The purpose of the foundation was to help disadvantaged youths, but Sandusky had used it as a cover to entice young men with perks and trips for a number of years. The charity folded.[3] At the same time, the issue remains of how to get institutions and communities to take action against popular sport heroes and coaches when they commit wrongs.[4]

A number of outstanding basketball stars have been devoting enormous efforts to helping others. **Eavin "Magic" Johnson** from the Los Angeles Lakers founded a development company in 1991 to offer entertainment to blighted inner-city neighborhoods. These fitness centers, homes, restaurants, and other services have revitalized their communities and in the process trained many black executives with necessary business skill and provided opportunities for their use (www.myhero.com).

Michael Jordan, who played mainly for the Chicago Bulls, has been supporting charities, including Boys' and Girls' Clubs of America and the Special Olympics. To join others in forty-one countries on the 2011 World Wish Day, April 29, organized by the Make-a-Wish Foundation to grant the wishes of children with life-threatening medical conditions, he gathered many well-known figures for Michael Jordan's Celebrity Charity Golf event (www. looktothestars.org).

Many athletes, such as **Andre Agassi** and others who founded **Athletes for Hope** in 2007, join together to facilitate others in their profession giving more to charity and inspiring people from all walks of life to volunteer and support their communities (www. athletesforhope.org). Agassi has been outstanding as a professional tennis player and as a supporter of charter schools, facilities for abused and neglected children, and for handicapped children.

Another top male tennis player. **Roger Federer** established the **Roger Foundation** to help disadvantaged children in 2003, especially for those in South Africa (where his mother is from). UNICEF appointed him Good Will Ambassador in 2006 to improve the lives of children globally.[5]

Andrea Jaeger retired as a top professional women's tennis player after she suffered injuries in 1987. Three years later, she co-founded the **Little Star Foundation** to help children with cancer

WIDESPREAD EFFORTS TO HELP
CHARITIES THROUGH SPORTS

Many people help others to enjoy sports through their schools and clubs. For example, the parents of **Tyler Ugolyn**, an investment analyst killed on 9/11, established a foundation in Ridgefield, Connecticut, to perpetuate their son's love of basketball. When Tyler had been a star of Columbia University's varsity basketball team, he founded a weekly basketball clinic in Harlem for local children. The foundation in his memory has joined with local organizations, cities, and others to renovate or build basketball courts from Houston to Detroit and beyond. Each one is named "Tyler's Court" and has a plaque saying. "I just love playing the game."[6]

You don't have to be a celebrity participate in a walkathon "fun run," or bike trek. Tens of thousands of "thons" have been collecting for schools, hospitals and homeless shelters. The largest "-thon" has been the **American Cancer Society's Relay for Life,** which raised more than $400 million in 2010. According to the *Wall Street Journal*, these grassroots efforts have become the favorite way to raise funds in the US.[7]

* * *

G. MULTIPURPOSE UMBRELLA ORGANIZATIONS

In order to maximize donor flexibility and achieve greater impact through combined funds, many people are giving in their communities through public-society benefit organizations, such as **United Ways**, as well as community foundations and donor-advised funds. They have access thereby to professionals in a wide variety of fields. If they choose to give within their own communities. They can work with people and groups they know personally. In addition, they don't have the expenses and administrative responsibilities required in individual or family foundations.

1. PUBLIC-SOCIETY BENEFIT ORGANIZATIONS

Public-society benefit organizations, according to the Center of Philanthropy at Indiana University, collect funds for redistribution to many kinds of charities, as well as organizations devoted to civil rights, voter education, public policy and social science research, and those focusing on community and neighborhood economic and civic development. They include many of the organizations listed in religious philanthropy, such as Catholic Charities, the Jewish Federations of North America, many Protestant denominations, and Moslem, Hindu, and Buddhist group.

UNITED WAY

The largest public-society benefit organization, United Way, has a network of about eighteen hundred community-based United Ways in forty-five countries and territories. Its major goals are to improve education, income stability, and health through giving funds, advocating, and volunteering in local communities. The organization was founded by a group of religious leaders in 1887 in Denver to bring people together to coordinate local services. This led to a single fundraising campaign for twenty-two agencies. By 1948, more than one thousand communities had established United Way organizations. Their national cooperative publicity efforts with the National Football League (NFL) enabled them to raise more than 1 billion in 1974, which surpassed the record of any other single organization up to that time.

An internal scandal broke out in 1992 when it was revealed that the long-serving president, **William Aramony**, had taken large sums of money for his own enrichment. This led to a serious probe and then reorganization. By 1994, *Financial World* magazine singled out United Way of America for its leadership in not-for-profit ethics and accountability. United Way then rebranded itself to be more than a "fundraiser" and to be known as the leading "community impact organization."

United Way has been expanding its programs constantly to reach more people through involving corporations, labor, unions, political advocates , and volunteers of all ages, as well as professionals (www.liveunited.org).

THE AMERICAN RED CROSS

Since its founding in 1881, the American Red Cross has been responding to emergencies - whether the care of war victims and the military or assisting people affected by devastating natural disasters. The Red Cross is also prominent in collecting, processing, and distributing lifesaving blood given by about four million people a year. The American Red Cross has more than half a million volunteers and thirty-five thousand employees in about seven hundred locally supported chapters. It depends on donations of time, money, and blood to be able to respond emergencies (www.redcross.org). The American organizations is also part of the **International Federation of Red Cross and Red Crescent Societies** (IFRC), which included about 186 national societies (www.ifrc.org).

2. COMMUNITY FOUNDATIONS

One of the best ways to have impact locally with large ramifications is to give through a community foundation. This enables you to design your own tax-deductible program with the board and staff of a group that is coordinating many activities within a specific city or region. The umbrella group for the approximately seven hundred US community foundations affirms that they "provide a simple, powerful, and highly personal approach to giving" (www. communityfoundations.net). Individuals, families, foundations, business, and organizations donate funds, which are then invested and distributed to community institutions. The American community foundations together manage about $40 billion in assets and distribute about $2 billion a year to various programs. The idea has also spread internationally to add another approximately one thousand such institutions in various countries.

The world's first community foundation was established in Cleveland in 1914 by banker **Frederic Goff** to pool the charitable resources available into an endowment and then to spend the interest on projects for the common good. Soon they created the "Emerald Necklace of the Cleveland Metroparks," spearheaded reforms in the public schools, supported equal education for girls, and started other programs. Within five years, community foundations were also established in Chicago, Boston, Milwaukee, Minneapolis, and Buffalo. Cleveland has remained one of the largest community foundations in the country with an endowment of over $1.8 billion. It has evolved from depending upon the wealthy to being supported by people from all income levels. It is committed "to serve as an active and visionary community agenda-setter, not a merge grant-maker" (www.clevelandfoundation.org).

The ten community foundations with the largest assets as of 2011, according to the Foundation Center, are Tulsa, Cleveland, Silicon Valley, the New York Community Trust, and then the institutions established in Chicago, California (Los Angeles), Greater Kansas City, Oregon, Marin Country, and San Francisco (www. foundationcenter.org).

To offer a few examples of what is being done, the largest group in **Tulsa,** with around $4,5 billion in assets, affirms that its approach is not to request support for a particular cause, but to ask potential contributors. "What is your cause?" It then provides professional assistance to identify the local institutions best able to carry out the donor's goals. Among their programs are funds for teachers, school supplies, emergency disaster relief, health and human services. And many more (www.tulsacf.org).

The **Silicon Valley Community Foundation,** with almost $1.8 billion in assets, draws upon its many successful entrepreneurs in the region to offer donors and corporations professional investment management to facilitate easy and effective ways to give locally, nationally, and internationally. Their grant-making strategies include economic security, education, immigrant integration, regional planning, and safety-net services. They also encourage venture philanthropy (www.siliconvalleycf.org).

The **New York Community Trust,** drawing upon more than $1.7 billion in assets, encourages people to contribute large and small amounts to be used in programs with a local focus so that there can be a lot of personal interaction. It can also eliminate the need and expense of private foundations and make it easier to encompass the desires of several generations. They support extensive programs, both large and small, in a multitude of areas, including health, education, and the arts (www.nycommunitytrust.org).

One of the most upbeat approaches to community foundations is offered by the one in **Utah.** For example, promotes its "Enlightened Entrepreneurs" program by saying it "doesn't think you need to have the bank account of a Gates to change the world." Instead, it urges people to come together to address Utah's complex social problems and thereby to create sustainable positive change. Among the many programs listed in its 2010 Annual Report, the emphasis is on the environment, education, human service, and advocacy and rights (www.utahcf.org). Fraser Nelson, the Executive Director, spearheaded the first "speed mentoring" event where social entrepreneurs from the state's most dynamic companies worked directly with nonprofits to find sustainable ways to generate revenue and to respond most effectively to community needs. This activity has been so successful, she told me, that it has been replicated by her community foundation in Utah and by similar groups in other states.[1]

3. DONOR-ADVISED FUNDS

One approach for a prospective donor who does not want the expense and effort to set up a private foundation is to contribute to a fund at an investment company, such as the Fidelity Charitable Gift Fund, which is the largest in the US. The contribution is irrevocable, but the donor gets to choose among different mutual funds on the investment side. He or she can only recommend which charities will receive their contributions since the fund makes the actual grants. The donor-advised funds have been especially attractive for people giving $1 million or less. Among the other firms handling them are Schwab and Vanguard. At the same time, many charities, such as the **National philanthropic trust** (www.nptrust.org), the **National Christian Foundation** (www.nationalchristian.com), **A Foundation of Philanthropic Funds** (www.fjc.org), **the Jewish Communal Fund** (www.jewishcommunalfund.org), the **U.S. Charitable Gift Trust** (www.worldwide.unitedway.org), offer their own donor-advised funds.

4. PROTECTING THE ENVIRONMENT AND ANIMALS

National Coalition to Save the Environment

To coordinate the efforts of twenty groups working to protect national air and water, forests and oceans wildlife, and climate, and to join international efforts for the environment, the Partnership Project was started in 1999 in Washington, D.C. Among the member group are American Rivers, Environment America, Friends of the Earth, Greenpeace, League of Conservation Voters, National Audubon Society, Pew Environment Group, National Parks Conservation Association, National Wildlife Federation, Physicians for Social Responsibility, Sierra Club, Union of Concerned Scientists, and the World Wildlife Fund (www.saveourenvironment.org).

Individuals can contribute greatly to the environment by supporting projects in their own communities. For example, **Kurt Landsberger** from Verona, New Jersey, and his late wife, **Anny,** have contributed over $100,000 to the **Essex Country Environment Center** to provide free field trips and transportation for over fifteen thousand students attending urban public school districts in Essex Country. "My wife and I always advocated for the environment," Mr. Landsberger said when he dedicated a tree in her memory at the center on June 27, 2011. "We started our business together, it was successful and we decided to use some of our profits to do what we could to educate children about the environment."[2]

Animal Advocacy Groups

Many animal lovers have joined together in different organizations to fight animal cruelty, adopt unwanted animals, and improve care for animals. The first humane society for these purposes was the **American Society for Prevention of Cruelty to Animals** (ASPCA) (www.aspca.org). **Equine Advocates** is active in protecting horses from abuse, rescuing maltreated horses, and educating people how to treat horses better (www.equineadvocates.org).

These examples make clear that a good way to start putting together your own program is first to check with various multi-purpose organizations to find out if they have suitable existing programs or if they can devise new ones to satisfy you within their own guidelines.

* * *

H. AWARDS TO HIGHLIGHT VALUES AND INSPIRE OTHERS

When you want to find and encourage the best and most innovation researchers and practitioners in the arts, sciences, and other fields or the best students at a school or university of your choice, a distinctive way to do so is to establish an award or prize that reflects the highest values of the institution or field and what you care about most. It is also a way to memorialize people important to you: family member, mentors, major personalities, et al. We immediately think of the Nobel Prizes in the sciences and peace, or the Pulitzer Prizes in journalism, but there are many others to consider as well.

Actually, Americans give more than five thousand major awards, with the great majority created since the late 1980s. Worldwide public and private philanthropies have been giving more than thirty thousand prizes annually with a value of more than $2 billion. It is evident that just giving money is only the beginning. So much depends on the selection process: who chooses and by what criteria, who administers the awards and at which institutions, according to **Dr. Larry E. Tise**, president of the **International Congress of Distinguished Awards** (ICDA) in Philadelphia (www.icda.org). He cautions that if the donor wants to achieve impact with the awards, he or she should be certain not to copy existing awards, but rather to find new fields and approaches.[1]

The **Nobel Prizes,** probably the best known in the world, have been given since 1901 for outstanding contributions in physics, chemistry, physiology or medicine, literature, and peace. They were established in the will of Alfred Nobel, the Swedish inventor of dynamite. Each prize brings a gold medal, a personal diploma, and a cash gift. An award in economics was added in 1968 (www.nobelprize.org).

Many of the most notable world figures have received the award. The medals have often served to spearhead greater appreciation for previously unrecognized groups of people. For example, the 2011 Nobel Peace Prize went to three female activists and political leaders for "their non-violent struggle for the safety of women and for women's rights" as peacemakers. The medalists were **President Ellen Johnson Sirleaf of Liberia Gbowee**, a Liberian social worker and peace activist; and **Twakkol Karman,** a Yemeni journalist and political activist. Ms. Karman, at thirty-two, is youngest Peace Prize laureate and the first Arab woman to receive the award. The Nobel committee indicated it hoped the prize would "help to bring on end to the suppression of women that still occurs in many countries."[2]

Albert and Mary Lasker, two Americans, established several awards in science and medicine beginning in 1945. Eighty of their awardees have gone on to win Nobel prizes.

Among the most prominent American awards are the **Pulitzer Prizes** begun in 1917 in journalism, letters and drama, education, and related fields. They were founded by the newspaper publisher **Joseph Pulitzer** and are administered by Columbia University. The Pulitzer Board has responded to cultural changes over the years by adding online journalism presentations beginning in 1999 and the widening of the music category in 1997 to include jazz and other mainstream musical forms (www.pulitzer.org).

The **Mac Arthur Fellows Program** grants "genius" awards to individuals of outstanding talents to encourage them to pursue their own creative, intellectual, and professional interests. Awardees may be writers, scientists, artists, social scientists, teachers, or people from many other fields. Each person receives $500,000 over five years. More than eight hundred US citizens or residents have received grants since 1981, about twenty to forty annually, and they have ranged in age from eighteen to eighty-two (www.macfound.org).

The **Ford Foundation,** in effect continuing this theme of rewarding creative innovators, in celebration of its seventy-fifth anniversary in 2011 gave Ford Foundation **Visionaries Awards** to twelve social innovators concerned with improved social and economic opportunities and participation for millions of marginalized people worldwide. Each of the one-time winners received $100,000 to continue his or her work (www.fordfoundation.org).

The **Bill & Melinda Gates Foundation** is also searching for innovation to fuel progress to solve global health and development dilemmas. Their **Grand Challenges Explorations** (GCE) program. started in 2008, is encouraging people worldwide to come up with one great idea and two pages to apply for a grant. Initial one-year grants amount to $100,000, but those with demonstrated success can request up to another $1 million (www.gatesfoundation.org).

The **X Prize Foundation** is also searching for radical break-throughs leading to new industries, genomic advances, space travel, and other of the world's Grand Challenges. They create and manage large-scale prize competitions to stimulate investment in research and development in four prize groups: education and global development, energy and environment, life sciences, and exploration. The X Prize

(501c3) Foundation is based in the US and led by **Dr. Peter H. Diamandis,** chairman and CEO, **Robert K. Weiss,** and a board of trustees, many drawn from other foundations (www.xprize.org). One of their prize areas with greatest impact has been DNA sequencing, suggested **by J. Craig Venter,** who created the first drafts of the other leading bioscience entrepreneurs.[3]

Meanwhile, **Paul Jacobs,** CEO of Qualcom, has joined with the X Prize Foundation in a $10 million competition for a non-invasive diagnostic smartphone that can detect health problems.[4]

Extraordinary vision also rewarded by the **Pritzker Architecture Prize,** but this time for design and innovation in new buildings created by leading architects. Since its inception in 1979 through the Hyatt Foundation, its outstanding winners from all over the world have included **Philip Johnson, Kevin Roche, I. M. Pei, Frank Gehry, Zaha Hadid**, and many more (www.pritzkerprize.com).

Since **Andre Carnegie** was such an outstanding philanthropist in establishing libraries and institutions to promote peace, the **Carnegie Medal of Philanthropy**, the most celebrated award in philanthropy, was established in 2001 to commemorate the centennial of Andrew Carnegie's business retirement and his efforts to give away his fortune in his lifetime. The medal selection committee brought together seven representatives from the twenty-three major institutions he had established, including Dr. **Vartan Gregorian**, president of the Carnegie Corporation of New York, the chair, Dr. **Jessica Matthews**, the president of the Carnegie Endowment for International Peace, and Dr. **Joel H. Rosenthal**, president of the Carnegie Council for Ethics in International Affairs. The medal, which is given every years, went in 2011 to such distinguished Americans as the Crown family, the Danforth family, Fiona and Stanley Druckenmiller, the Lauder family, Pamela and Pierre Omidyar, the Pew family, and the Pritzker family (www.carnegiemedals.org).

The **National Committee on American Foreign Policy** under the leadership of its President, **Dr. George D. Schwab** gives a series of awards to outstanding Americans and others who have contributed to resolving conflicts that threaten American interests and the international community. The notable recipients of the

Hans J. Morgenthau Award include David Rockefeller, Henry Kissinger and Colin L. Powell; those for the George F. Kennan Award for Distinguished Public Service include Cyrus R. Vance, Paul A. Volcker and Richard C. Holbrooke.[5]

An extraordinary example of establishing a prize to proclaim a donor's central values is the Ibrahim Prize established by Sudanese telecommunication mogul Dr. Mo Ibrahim in 2007. The award goes to a democratically elected former African executive head of state or government who has served his term in office within the term limits set by the country's constitution, has left office within the previous three years, and has demonstrated excellence in office. As the prize consists of $5 million over ten years and then $200,000 annually for life, it is the biggest one in the world (www.moibrahimfoundation. org). The 2011 prize went to the president of the Republic of Cape Verde, Pedro Verona Pires, who became prime minister in 1975 after winning independence for his country from the Portuguese. In 1991, he accepted defeat during the first democratic elections, but then regained power in 2001 and continued until he stepped down voluntarily in 2011.[6]

Since the purpose of this book is to demonstrate that giving is not just for the very rich, creating and giving awards and prizes can be worthwhile to recognize extraordinary attainments and accomplishments, to encourage worthy recipients to continue their efforts, and to inspire others to follow the awardee's examples. This can apply to every college and university, to K-12 educational institutions. To art, music, literature programs, scientific discoveries, and engineering innovations. Awards reinforce inspirational values for students, scholars. scientists, and artists, as well as all people interested in a particular field and everyone attending a ceremony or hearing about it in the media.

How do you establish an award or prize? The most direct way is to see what prizes your alma mater gives at graduation exercises and to determine if there would be room for what you have in mind. Especially a unique, original award that would add a new dimension to an institution or create something entirely different.

Some institutions may welcome many prizes and not have a high minimum amount for the contribution. Others may wish a commitment for a certain time period (five years? a lifetime? An endowment?). The negotiation process for establishing and administering an award is very important for eliciting the views of both the door and the institution. The donor will want to follow the interpretation of the award and the selection of the recipients very closely over time since the administrators at the institution may change and the new ones may bring different interpretations about the award's significance. If the disagreements are really acute, the donor may decide to discontinue the award or go elsewhere to give it. When the donor feels passionately about a certain cause or issue, it is important to be certain his or her values are reflected in the award. At the same time, the institution has the right to protect its own values and reputation in presenting a prize.

If the sum of money given is substantial enough, you may want to establish an independent foundation, a board, and an administrative staff to select the winners and then to award the prizes. This is really justified only when the award approaches the size of the Nobel Prizes. Otherwise, the large sums required for administration could be spent better in helping research, development, or whatever else the award is celebrating.

I started in the "awards business" at the age of nine when I assisted my father in presenting distinguished service medals at the City College of the City New York (CCNY) and the Alpha Epsilon Pi fraternity (see the introduction). Once I began earning a living, I established awards to highlight achievements at the institutions closest to me. My earliest awards at an educational institution was designated specifically for women since I had experienced so much discrimination as a woman in my early years. Ironically, the institution ignored the award's purpose as started in the endowment and chose a man since probably they were accustomed to choosing men automatically. When I called their attention to the mistake, they rectified the situation by choosing a competent woman.

The late president of the **Center for the Study of the Presidency, Dr. R. Gordon Hoxie,** asked me to establish an award program for the best student essays from colleges all over the country. From 1980 to 2002, we awarded ten (and sometimes more when there were ties) to students from great universities and small colleges. The institutions included the service academies, like West Point and the Air Force Academy, and smaller denominational colleges. The awards were made at our annual student conference in Washington, where we heard top American and international leaders, including Presidents Ronald Reagan and Bill Clinton, Supreme Court judges, senators, cabinet officials, and others. I was proud to participate in this great educational effort in democracy and civil society.

At the **Columbia School of International and Public Affairs (SIPA)**, I established the **Dr. Susan Aurelia Gitelson Award for Human Values in international Affairs** in 1980 in memory of my father and originally in his name. Through the years, we have had the most extraordinary awardees from all over the world in human rights, sustainable development, and many other fields. This has become the oldest award SIPA gives, and I have endowed it in perpetuity.

Meanwhile, the founder of the **Columbia Institute for Human Rights, Professor Louis Henkin,** asked me to establish a human rights essay award, which for many years (1987-2006) was the sole award given to the extraordinary students who often had risked their lives to fight for human rights in their home countries and then had come to Columbia to get a more formal legal and intellectual grounding in the discipline and to network with other human rights advocates from around the world. Many of the winners of the award have gone on to successful careers as law professors and heads of human rights institutions.

Probably the most significant award I established was the **Gitelson Peace Prize** at the **Harry S. Truman Research Institute for the Advancement of Peace** of the Hebrew University of Jerusalem. I conceived the prize in 1989 at an optimistic time in the long process of middle East peace negotiations with the idea that Jerusalem has always been the object of peace players for Jews. Christians, and Moslems, and a peace symbol throughout the world. Despite some diplomatic difficulties, we were able to award the prize in Jerusalem in 1991 to the President of the European Parliament, the **Hon. Simone Veil** of France. Subsequently, the Truman Institute received more substantial funding and transformed the award into the **Truman Peace Prize,** which has been awarded to notable contributors to peace negotiations mainly in the US. These have included Norwegian Foreign Minister Johan Jorgen Holst, Senator George J. Mitchell, Jr., UN Ambassador Richard C. Holbrooke, General Colin L. Powell (ret.), Ambassador Dennis B. Ross, and the Hon. James D. Wolfensohn.

After the "man of my life". **Jerome ("jerry") Meyerowitz,** died in 1991, I immediately established the **Gitelson Meyerowitz Distinguished Service Award** in his memory at the **Sutton Place Synagogue** where we had met. Through the years, we have honored the heads of Jewish educational institutions, museums, defense organizations. Umbrella organizations, rabbis, and other exemplary people. This has enabled nonprofit institution leaders to tell synagogue members about their organizations and alert people about places and groups they would want to visit and join.

From my very positive experiences in giving awards, I encourage you to consider establishing an award to honor or memorialize someone important to you while furthering constructive and innovative activities to improve the world. As with everything else, though, it is important to think through carefully what you want to do and where you can do this most effectively.

* * *

I. INTERNATIONAL AID TO ENCOURAGE SELF-RELIANCE AND SUSTAINABLE DEVELOPMENT

When you hear about child hunger in an African or Asian country, you may be tempted to send a contribution to any organization that says it is feeding the children. But it is so important to research the problem and the available charities very carefully before sending money to some far-off place. A prominent example occurred when **Greg Mortenson** wrote *Three Cups of Tea* (2006) about his efforts to build schools in Pakistan and Afghanistan through the Center Asia Institute he had directed, but it was alleged in 2011 that he used most of the funds he raised for himself and that few schools were actually built. Since it is often difficult to examine specific projects in a remote country by yourself, fortunately there are quite a few resource centers for international philanthropy that can help ensure your contribution will be used be used for the maximum benefit of the intended recipients. In addition, it is helpful to have expert reports comparing development efforts within a single country and among different countries.

The most comprehensive guide is the **Charities Aid Foundation America (CAF America),** which manages more than $4 billion for charities worldwide and already deals with more than one hundred thousand organizations already eligible with them. They have distributed more than $100 million in donor funds to over twenty-five hundred foreign nonprofit organizations in more than seventy-six countries. Individuals, communities, corporations, and others who wish to become donors can get necessary information about purposes and activities of various charities, their degree of transparency, the amount of risk, and other considerations. If they still can't find what they seek, CAF America, which is located in Alexandria, Virginia, will help them to develop new programs. They have professional dealing with tax questions, making grants, and measuring impact. At the same time, foreign nonprofits can turn to them to become eligible to receive grants. Donors pay CAF America an administrative fee for international grant-making and advisory services, while recipients also pay for advice. Among the main concerns are improving education, health, the environment, and the arts (www.cafamerica.org).

Another umbrella organization, **InterAction,** based in Washington. D.C., brings together around two hundred US based non-governmental organizations (NGOs) to work internationally on such major issues as poverty reduction, sustainable development, disaster response, refugee protection, and gender equality. Their member organizations represent many religious-based, disease-eradication, and economic development groups (www.interaction.org).

Grantmakers Without Borders, located in San Francisco, emphasize capacity-building support for international grant makers for the global "South" or less-development countries. About one hundred and sixty individual donors, private foundations, and private charities join to assist education, community, and collaboration among international social change grant makers. They "value and respect the wisdom and experience of local communities in all their diversity" and wish to amplify "the voice of the global South in international philanthropy" (www.gwob.net).

The **Rotary International** network is made up of more than thirty-three thousand Rotary clubs in over two hundred countries and geographical areas. There are approximately 1.2 million business and professional members who volunteer their time and abilities to serve their own communities and the world. They support the Rotary Foundation, which endeavors "to advance world understanding through the improvement of health, the support of education, and the alleviation of poverty." The nonprofit foundation gets its support from voluntary contributions from Rotarians and others who share its vision. Their programs include financing wells and other necessities in rural villages, improving the environment, providing scholarships, and their number-one goal of eradicating polio. Since they began their PolioPlus program in 1985, over two billion children have received the oral polio vaccine (www.rotary.org).

People who are interested in particular parts of the world can turn to groups like the **International Child Resource Institute-Africa (ICRI)**, which is part of the international institute based in Berkeley, California. The East African affiliate established an office in Nairobi in 2005, which is run and operated by Kenyans who have local and international experience, in the efforts to improve lives for children and families. The ICRI also has programs in other African countries (www.icriafrica.org).

Since 2001, **Give2Asia** has been bringing together donors from business and nonprofits, especially the Asia Foundation, to grant $150 million in its first ten years to reach China, India, Indonesia, Japan, Cambodia, and other countries with an emphasis on education, health, disaster, social services, and environment (www. give2asia.org).

When you have access to so many organizations, how do you choose where to put your efforts? The **Innovations for Poverty**

Action has done rigorous studies of what works in fighting poverty through randomized controlled trials led by researchers from Harvard, Yale, MIT, and other lending universities. They have been evaluating actual development efforts, such as microfinance, education, health, and agriculture. The approach is explained further in *More Than Good Intentions: How a New Economics Is Helping to Solve Global Poverty* by Dean Karlan and Jacob Appel.[1] The authors apply behavioral economics in their research in villages in Africa, Asia, and Latin America to show ways to improve banking, insurance, education, and other programs to vastly benefit the lives of poor people everywhere (www.poverty-action.org).

A major force for increasing development possibilities globally has been **Professor Jeffrey D. Sachs,** director of the Earth Institute at Columbia University. He worked with then **UN Secretary-General Kofi Annan** and others internationally on formulating the **Millennium Development Goals (MDGs)** in 2000 to reduce extreme poverty, disease, and hunger by the year 2015. The main goals are: cut extreme poverty and hunger by half, achieve universal primary education, promote gender equality and empower women, reduce child mortality by two-thirds, reduce maternal mortality by three quarters, combat HIV/AIDS, malaria, and other diseases, ensure environmental sustainability, and promote a global partnership for development.

To implement these goals, Sachs served as director of the **UN Millennium Project** from 2002 to 2006. When I asked him at the Carnegie Council on Ethics and International Affairs in 2011 how effective he thought the MDGs had been, he replied that they have organized ways for civil societies all over the world to hold governments to account. In addition, he cited the malaria vaccine as an advance in controlling communicable diseases. "People are alive by the millions now," he said. "because of this." He added, "We are seeing farmers grow more food because of the ability to use higher-yield varieties and more scientific approaches for the first time. "He also noted "there is a tremendous spread of ideas, knowledge engagement, community development" around the world.[2]

Sachs also joined with **Ray Chambers,** a private-equity investor, in 2005 to establish the **Millennium Promise Alliance**. Their key program is the **Millennium Villages Project** organized with host countries, local governments, and civil society organizations in the communities and countries where the project would be implemented. They continue to work closely with UN Secretary-General Ban Ki-moon (www.milleniumpromise.org). The alliance draws upon the Earth Institute's scientific research to find solutions for sustainable development in face of the world's most difficult problems, including climate change, poverty, disease, and the proper use of resources (www.earth.columbia.edu).

One of the best ways to improve the quality of development programs is for their participants to communicate directly with others facing the same or similar challenges. **South-South News** is a digital platform that was launched at the UN in 2010 to advance implementation of the Millennium Development Goals through sharing positive news and good practices among developing countries in the "South" (particularly in Latin America, the Caribbean, Africa, Asia and the Pacific, the Middle East, and East Europe regions) with each other and with industrialized countries (www.southsouthnews.com).

Progress in development depends so much on global literacy and gender equality in education. John Wood established **Room to Read** in 2000 out of the belief that "World Change Starts with Educated Children." The goal has been to transform the lives of millions of children in collaboration with local communities, partner organizations, and governments by building libraries and schools and filling them with books. Where materials did not exist in certain languages, Wood and his team published them. By 2011, they had opened twelve thousand libraries and fifteen hundred schools and had given out ten million books in Vietnam, Cambodia, Nepal, South Africa, Zambia, and many other countries. Wood draws upon his experiences as a Microsoft executive to run Room to Read like a business rather than a charity. In twenty years, he hopes to have "100,000 libraries, reaching fifty million kids," he told Nicholas D. Kristof when they met in Vietnam.[3]

The emphasis on self-reliance is evident in the new **Stanford Institute for Innovation in Developing Economies,** sponsored with a gift in 2011 of $150 million from **Robert E. and Dorothy**

King. They felt "the university can make our money more fruitful than we can on our own," according to Mrs. King. **Professor Hau Lee**, the institute's head, said, "Many people are doing relief or aid operations, but at the institute, we will be asking how we can stimulate entrepreneurs and business ideas so than the people receiving aid today can become self-sufficient, so they won't need aid in the future."[4]

One of the leading research programs for international development was sponsored by **James D. Wolfensohn,** the former president of the World Bank, from 2006 to 2011 at the **Bookings Institution** in Washington, D.C. The **Wolfensohn Center for Development** did rigorous research on major topics, such as how to lift people out of poverty and create a better future for today's youth. This has led to the weaving of development and global poverty issues, including foreign aid effectiveness, into a series of initiatives across Brookings, particularly the Global Economy and Development program. IN addition, the Center's Middle East Youth Initiative has led to a new phase working closely with partners in the region (www. brookings.edu).

It is evident that anyone desiring to help people in other countries can find out what really can be done by turning to the charity directories, research studies, and actual field work reports delineated in this chapter. If you want to be effective, you must have a grasp of what has already been done and an awareness of the most successful approaches being tried.

* * *

IV.

HOW TO EVALUATE CHARITIES

Once you have probed your own values and passions and considered giving to potential charities, research and scrutinize them to be certain that they are going to maximize your contributions for the designated causes. Fortunately, there are a number of easily accessible websites where you can look up many of the approximately 1.6 million existing charities.

Let us first discuss basic considerations for giving wisely. Then we will provide a list of key watchdog groups to scrutinize and evaluate various charities. Finally, we will provide references to additional websites for people who really want to dig deeply.

A. HOW TO RESEARCH AND EVALUATE POTENTIAL GIVING OPPORTUNITIES

GUIDING PRINCIPLES FOR GIVING WISELY

1) Find out all you can about the organizations that serve your cause(s) and compare them. What are their goals? Programs? Results? You can request written information about the charity and their latest annual report, including their mission statement, a list of the board of directors. Who is guiding their investments and where are they putting their funds?

2) Be careful of scams, such as organizations that choose names close to those of genuine charities. Check their websites. Be especially wary in times of crises, e.g., groups after Hurricane Katrina in 2005 that put "Katerina" in their domain names to get unsuspecting people to donate to them.

3) Be certain they are sufficiently transparent about their administration and fundraising expenses. Find out what proportion of the funds they raise goes to actual program services it should be 65 to 75 percent unless it is a new or very small charity with large expenses. Salaries and fundraising costs generally should take up no more than

25 percent. Beware of nepotism, especially when it comes to controlling financial resources.

4) Check that they have tax-exempt status under section 501(c)(3) of the Internal Revenue Code. Will Your contribution be tax-deductible (which is not always the same thing)?

5) Do not be pressured into donating. In addition, be careful not to respond immediately to an emotional appeal. You have the right to request written information about the charity and time to think about what you wish to do. Be especially wary of phone solicitations by telemarketers who receive a percentage of the money they raise. If you want to give to that group, better to end the conversation and donate directly to the charity on its website so that it will get all the funds.

6) Keep written records of your donations and expect written receipts from the charity. Do not give your credit card or bank account number over the phone or online unless you are certain about the charity's identity.

7) Check if the charity is registered by federal, state, and/or local authorities. This ensures that the charities will file financial information with government authorities, although it does not guarantee government approval of the charity.

8) Do not feel obliged to send a donation to a charity if it sends you gifts, such as greeting cards, through the mails. You do not have to send a payment for unordered merchandise. The money they ask for goes mainly to cover the cost of the solicitation mailing. In addition, the charity is likely to sell your name to other charities for their fundraising campaigns.

9) Check out the result of the charity's efforts both by asking them and by researching reports about by on the Internet, especially through the watchdog agencies. If possible, visit the charity and volunteer your services so that you have a very good idea of what they are actually doing.

10) Don't divide your contributions among too wide a variety of organizations. When you are satisfied with your research, concentrate your giving on only a few charities, speak to

their leaders, and make long-term commitments to them so that you can have maximum impact. As you become a regular supporter, keep scrutinizing the charities to be certain they continue to achieve maximum effectiveness.

* * *

B. THE MAIN WATCHDOG AGENCIES

Fortunately, there are several agencies that evaluate major charities and offer their recommendations on their websites. They can help you determine how your contributions can be most effective. Among the chief agencies are:

1) **Charity Navigator** (www.charitynavigator.org) evaluates over fifty-five hundred of American's biggest charities in terms of their transparency, accountability, effectiveness, etc.

2) **Better Business Bureau** (www.bbb.org) BBB Wise Giving Alliance Standards for Charity Accountability (give.org) also provides extensive evaluation criteria.

3) **GuideStar** (www.guidestar.org) has a data base of 1.8 million nonprofit and lists all tax-exempt organizations registered with the IRS.

4) **Great Nonprofits** (www.greatnanprofits.org) works with GuideStar and other evaluators by gathering reviews from people who have personal experience with various charities.

5) **The Independent Sector** (www.independentsector.org) which is made up to approximately six hundred organizations, has developed Charting Impact (www.chartingimpact.org) with their members, BBB Wise Giving Alliance, and doing GuideStar USA to evaluate what charities are doing and accomplishing by asking five seemingly simple questions:

   a) What is your organizations trying to accomplish?
   b) What are your strategies for making this happen?
   c) What are your organization's capabilities for doing this?

d) How will your organization know if you are making process?

e) What have you and haven't you accomplished so far?

The reports are then available online with all the sponsoring organizations for potential funders and partners.

6) **Give Well** evaluates and ranks charities in depth by categories (www.givewell.org). They focus on "how well programs actually work" i.e., their effects on the people they serve.

7) **American Institute of Philanthropy** (www.charitywatch.org) rates over five hundred charities based on their rating system.

* * *

C. OTHER INFORMATION AND EVALUATION SOURCES

1) **The Council on Foundations** works to increase the effectiveness and accountability of its seventeen hundred grant-making foundations and corporate members (www. cof.org).

2) **Social Impact Research** (www.rootcause.org/socialimpact-research) gathers and analyzes data to assist social impact funders and donors identify and support "the most effective, efficient, and sustainable organization working to solve social problems."

3) **The Center for High Impact Philanthropy of the School of Social Policy and Practice at the University of Pennsylvania** draws on academic research, nonprofits financial and performance data, site visits, and interviews of practitioners to locate high impact opportunities (www. impact.upenn.edu).

4) **National Center for Charitable Statistics of the Urban Institute** collects data on organizations management,

resources, development campaigns, etc. (www.nccsdataweb.urban.org).

5) **The Standards for Excellence Institute at the Maryland Association of Nonprofit Organizations** promotes the highest standards of ethics and accountability in nonprofits (www.standardsforexcellenceinstitute.org).

6) **The Evangelical Council for Financial Accountability** accredits Christian ministries, churches, educational institutions, and other tax-exempt organizations on the basis of its standards for financial accountability, governance, and fundraising (www.ecfa.org).

7) **JustGive.org** has a database of about 1.8 million charities and singles out one thousand of them that have met stringent public requirements. It indicates that this should enable you to find the charities you desire to support and then give to them securely through its website (www.justgive.org).

8) **Social Programs That Work** based their suggestions for social policy initiatives on rigorous research in many fields such as education, health, and international development (www.evidencebasedprograms.org).

9) **The Center for What Works** researches nonprofit programs and indicators for their success in fields such as community organizing, performing arts, and youth mentoring (www.whatworks.org).

You should be able to find the sectors and organizations you wish and to evaluate them by consulting one or more of these websites. If someone has solicited your aid for an organization that is not rated favorably by these knowledgeable groups then be wary about contributing. At the least, go back to the groups to have them answer the key evaluation questions listed above.

* * *

V.

CHOICES AND COMMITMENTS—
HOW WILL YOUR CONTRIBUTIONS
HAVE THE GREATEST IMPACT

A. DIVERSIFY BUT FOCUS!

Exploring various causes and options for devoting yourself to helping others can be overwhelming! There are so many organizations out there in just about every category: combating diseases, educating young people, higher education, the arts, science, global aid, social venture investing, as well as umbrella organizations, offering possibilities at the local, national, and global levels. What can you do?

1) Consider your values and what appeals to you most, especially if you are searching for long-term involvement.
2) Make lists of the organizations that appear as if they are dealing with your major causes and do careful research to find out what they are actually doing, who their leaders are, and what successes and failures they have had so far.
3) Diversity the institutions and causes you support so you won't become overly entwined with any one group.
4) On the other hand, once you have made your selection, focus your efforts closely with the groups you have top priority for you.
5) Develop personal relations with lay leaders and staff; find out where you can be active; join a committee and, if possible, the board so that you have a clear perspective on the group and its effectiveness.
6) Re-evaluate the organization after one year, five years, and then ten in terms of your long-term commitments.
7) Decide on the basis of both experience and reflection where you want to concentrate your efforts and funds while you are alive and who should be the main beneficiaries in your will.
8) Give money for a pilot project, especially if you have only limited resources, so that, if it is successful, it can be supported by more substantial organizations.[1]

* * *

B. QUESTIONS FOR MAKING YOUR CHOICES, ESPECIALLY IF YOU WANT TO ESTABLISH YOUR OWN PROJECTS AND PROGRAMS

After you have examined your values and goals and researched what various organizations are doing, you will be ready to choose how to concentrate your efforts to build on your passions for maximum effectiveness. Consider these choice:

> Do you want to be active on the local, national, or global level?
> If local, you can work with people face to face and really get to know them.
> If national, you can build networks and reach more people
> If global, you can think and act more strategically.

Can you be most effective by working for a nonprofit organization or will this force you to devote more time than you would like to administration, fundraising, etc.? Would you prefer the freedom of being an independent supporter for ongoing activities or to special projects and programs you devise with the group's leaders?

Do you feel you can achieve your goals by joining an existing organization or do you feel no one is doing what you feel is necessary and you want to start your own organization? If the latter, how much and what resources can you contribute? Who will help you carry out your goals?

How many recipient organizations do you want to deal with? If there are too many, your efforts may be too diffuse. It is better to focus on one, two, or three, At the same time, never commit all your efforts and resources to only one organization because circumstances may vary-most obviously, when the leaders change. The new director may have an entirely different perspective and may want to bring in a whole new staff. He or she may even shunt you aside as unnecessary for the new approach. If you feel uncomfortable in the new situation, you want to be able to move elsewhere as soon as you feel it is necessary.

Do you want to have an open-ended commitment to a certain organization or do you want to set yourself time limits, e.g., five to ten years or certain goals have been achieved?

When combating a disease (e.g., prostate cancer), do you want to concentrate on basic research to find the causes and possible cures for it? Or would you prefer to concentrate on aiding patients who are already suffering from a disease (e.g., breast cancer)?

When you give, do you want name recognition, especially since your contributions will show your values very clearly and possibly attract others to join you, or do you prefer to give anonymously? The institution may want to identify you, even if you began by giving anonymously, as **Marian University in Indian** did when **Michael A. Evans** gave them $48 million. Since they wanted his gift to encourage others, they set up the Michael A. Evans Center for Health Service.[2]

* * *

C. WHAT DETERMINES "SUCCESS"

How do you know if the organization or program you are supporting is a "success"?

If you begin with a strategic plan and clear goals, you can examine if you are moving in the right direction after six months, a year, or ten years. It is especially helpful if you have measurable data that can be quantified and compared. Unfortunately, such data is expensive to collect and is not readily available, so precise measurement is usually practical only on large projects with substantial funding.

In most situations, you can rely mainly on qualitative tests or measures:

Is the organization contributing to the values you have established and visibly solving the problems it has pinpointed?

What other groups are grappling with the same or similar issues? Are they using the same or related techniques?

What have they learned that might be applicable to your program? Where do they seem to have problems that you appear to have overcome or solved?

If there have been failures along the way, have they been analyzed thoroughly so that lessons can be applied in other situations?

In talking with the grantees and the people who are supposed to be helped, do they show evidence that they are advancing? Do they express satisfaction with their experiences?

If a consultant has come in to start a new enterprise, has he or she trained local people to be able to carry on the enterprise by themselves, especially after the consultant leaves?

If the aim is training and education, have the trainees and students advanced to a higher professional level? Is there need to remedy some problems?

If you have established an award, are the awardees going on in their fields of expertise? Are they inspiring others to follow them?

If you are donating seed money for a new program at a certain institution, are others, especially large foundations, joining in with more substantial contributions?

Do you want to give away most or all of your money during your own lifetime?

Do you instead want to include future generations in our programs or foundation? If so, have you been teaching them to give to others from a young age and observing their progress? As you set out the goals for your foundation, will you restrict them only to your own passions or will they be flexible enough to respond to the causes of your children and grandchildren?

After all your study and reflection, you are ready to take action. You will enjoy giving to benefit others and thereby also enhance your own life!

* * *

Appendix:

Donor-Advised Funds, Trusts, and Foundation

To define the purpose of their philanthropy and to maximize tax-deduction advantages, many people turn to Donor-Advised Funds, Trusts, Foundation, and other vehicles, which we will describe briefly.

DONOR-ADVISED FUNDS

As delineated in our multi-purpose organizations chapter, you can donate funds to a community foundation or to stock brokers like Fidelity and Schwab who provide such tax exempt opportunities. When you donate money, you receive an immediate tax deduction. You can then "recommend" to the funds how much it should donate to which charity and when. Since the donor advises where the money should go, the fund acts like a foundation without the administrative costs. One drawback, however, is that the donor cannot take his funds back it he later wants to use them for himself.

CHARITABLE TRUSTS

These are legal vehicles for giving charity in the form of money or property, while at the same time passing on principal and income to your children or other designated heirs. The two major kinds are charitable lead trusts where the charity comes first in distributing funds and the charitable remainder trust where the income goes first to your children or heirs and the remaining funds to the charity.

PLANNED GIVING OR POOLED INCOME FUND

The donor gives a certain amount of money to a recognized nonprofit institution and then receives a certain percentage as income for the rest of his or her lifetime. After the death of the donor, the charity keeps the funds.

FOUNDATIONS

If a donor has assets to contribute of at least $1 million a year, then it may be worth the effort to establish a private or family foundation with all the administrative and legal expenses if entails. This is especially appealing for people who want to train their children and grandchildren in philanthropy, although it is wisest to let the children and grandchildren participate in allocation decisions. The foundation may make grants to the charities it chooses and is obligated by IRS to give at least 5 percent of its income annually for programs and administration. Alternatively, an operating foundation provides charitable services directly and makes few, if any grants, to outside organizations. It may deduct up to 50 percent of its adjusted gross income.

Generally, a foundation is "a non-government entity that is established as a nonprofit corporation or a charitable trust, with a principal purpose of making grants to unrelated organizations, institutions, or individuals for scientific, educational, cultural, religious, or other charitable purposes." A private foundation, such as the Ford or Rockefeller Foundations, derives its money from a family, an individual, or a corporation. A public foundation, or a grant-making public charity, receives its resources from different sources, such as foundations, individuals and government agencies. Most community foundations are also grant-making public charities (www.grantspace.org).

NOTES

I. INTRODUCTION: GIVING BENEFITS OTHERS AND YOURSELF

1) Arthur Brooks, "Why Giving Makes You Happy." *The New York Sun,* December 28, 2007.
2) www.apa.org, February 2003.
3) *New York Times (NYT),* October 30, 2011.
4) Table showing US GDP percentages 1969-2009 in Giving USA, 2010, p.17.
5) Giving USA Foundation 2010 Executive Summary, The Center on Philanthropy at Indiana University, pp. 6-7.
6) *USA Today,* June 25, 2007.
7) *NYT,* December 19, 2005.
8) Giving USA Foundation, 2010, pp.4-5
9) Giving USA Foundation, 2010, p. vii.
10) Giving USA Foundation, 2010, pp. vii, 18.
11) Based on our conversation, December 8,2011.

II. DIFFERENT KINDS OF IMPASSIONED GIVING FOR MAXIMUM EFFECT

A. Wealthiest Donors who are Pacesetters

1) *Forbes,* June 6, 2011.
2) *NYT,* October 24, 2011.
3) *Forbes,* October 10, 2011.
4) *NYT,* July 6, 2006.
5) *Financial Times,* December 9, 2011.

6) *Forbes*, June 6, 2011.
7) *Fortune*, July 10, 2006.
8) Philanthropy.com, February 6, 2011.
9) *Wall Street Journal (WSJ)*, August 4, 2011.
10) *Forbes*, June 6, 2011.
11) The Princeton Club of New York, Club Notes, May 2011.
12) *WSJ*, April 21, 2006.
13) www.seattletimes.nwsource.com.
14) www.mashable.com, September 24, 2010.
15) www.mashable.com, December 9, 2010.

B. Innovative Givers for Meaningful Causes

1) *NYT*, December 20, 2011.
2) www.bloomberg.com, May 11, 2010.
3) quoted in www.en.wikipedia.org.
4) Gully Wells, "The Woman in white," Vogue, March 2011, pp. 536 and 571.
5) *WSJ*, June 17, 2011.
6) *WSJ*, May 10, 2011.
7) *WSJ*, September 29, 2011.
8) www.nytimes.com, September 9, 2010.
9) Philanthropy.com, February 6, 2011.
10) *WSJ*, June 29, 2011

C. Social Entrepreneurs who Strive for Impact

1) Online.wsj.com, June 30, 2011.
2) Philanthropy.com. February 6, 2011.
3) More details are available in Matthew Bishop and Michael Green's *Philanthropcapitalism: How Giving Can Save the World*, New York, 2008.
4) *NYT*, January 8, 2008.
5) New York, 2008.
6) *NYT*, June 23, 2011.

7) For a more extensive examination of the Acumen Fund, see Helen Coster's "Can Venture Capital Save the World," *Forbes*, December 19, 2011, pp 66-75. In the same issue, Forbes also features another twenty-nine social entrepreneurs who are tackling the world's most intractable problems, pp. 78-84

8) See David A. Kaplan, "The 2011 Businessperson of the year, "Fortune, December 12, 2011, pp. 100-114.

9) *WSJ*, October 10, 2011.

10) www.mercurynews.com, October 7, 2011.

11) *WSJ*, December 1, 2011.

12) Philanthropy.com, November 9, 2011.

D. Celebrities who Promote Giving to Others

1) New York, 2007.

2) Philanthropytoday.com, August 14, 2011.

3) Online.barrons.com, December 6, 2010.

4) www.wikipedia.org.

E. Government Officials and Nonprofit Professionals

1) Private e-mail, October 9, 2011.

2) www.cbsnews.com and private e-mail from Robert M. Morgenthau, transmitted by his administrative assistant, Ida VanLindt, December 21, 2011.

3) *Fortune*, September 26, 2011.

4) *NYT,* November 27, 2011.

5) *Insidenypl,* Fall 2011.

6) *NYT*, October 6, 2010.

7) *NYT*, October 11, 2011.

8) *WSJ*, May 16, 2011.

9) *WSJ*, October 20, 2011.

F. Volunteers who Help in Many Imaginative Ways

1) Based on surveys conducted by the U.S. Census Bureau for the Bureau of Labor Statistics, as quoted by The *Chronicle of Philanthropy*, www.philanthropy.com, August 9, 2011.
2) *NYT*, May 9, 2011.

G. Social Media Networkers for Good Causes

1) Bloomberg Businessweek, October 25-31, 2010.
2) NYT, August 18, 2011.
3) www.philanthropy.com. November 23, 2011.
4) For the full breakdown, see www.blackbaud.com.
5) www.philanthropy.com, October 6, 2011.

III. MAJOR AREAS FOR GIVING

A. Religious Philanthropy

1) www.theblaze.com, July 21, 2011.
2) According to the World bank, philanthropy.com, July 5, 2011.
3) The Associated Press, quoted in philanthropy.com, September 2, 2011.
4) Also see NYT, June 14, 2011.
5) Private e-mail from Mark D. Medin, senior vice president, UJA-Federation of the New York, December 22, 2011.
6) Interview with Fred Schwartz, July 7, 2011.

B. Improving Education K-12

1) *WSJ*, August 20-21, 2011, p.C5.
2) *NYT*, June 19, 2008.
3) *NYT*, June 19, 2008.
4) www.philanthropy.com, February 6, 2011.
5) *WSJ*, July 18, 2011.
6) Education Update Online, April 2007.

7) "The Chronicle of Philanthropy," *Philanthropy Today*, August 24, 2011.
8) *WSJ*, July 27, 2011.
9) *WSJ*, April 2-3, 2011.
10) Private e-mail from Zina Greene, December 3, 2011.
11) *WSJ*, June 15, 2011.
12) *WSJ*, June 23, 2011.
13) *WSJ*, July 6, 2011.
14) *WSJ*, April 29, 2011.
15) "Philanthropy 50," *Chrn of Phil*, February 6, 2011.
16) *WSJ*, July 19, 2011.

C. Higher Education

1) **www.college.columbia.edu,** Sept. 8, 2010.
2) *WSJ*, November 18, 2011
3) *NYT*, Oct. 1, 1995.
4) www.rockwithjudaism.com/2010/12.
5) www.library.yale.edu, Oct. 2007.
6) *NYT*, March 21, 2006.

D. Science and Health

1) *NYT*. October 16. 2011.
2) *NYT*. November 12, 2011.
3) *WSJ*, November 9, 2011.
4) *WSJ*, March 28, 2011.
5) *WSJ*, September 20, 2011.
6) *WSJ*, August 4, 2011.
7) *WSJ*, June 22, 2011.
8) *WSJ*, July 13, 2011.
9) Philanthropy.com/article/No-18.
10) Advertisement in the *NYT*, July 10, 2011.
11) www.syracuse.com, July 28, 2011.
12) *NYT*, September 22, 2011.

E. Arts, Culture, and Humanities

1) *NYT*, June 18, 2011.
2) www.nytimes.com, October 19, 2011.

F. Sport

1) See many other examples in www.lookotherstars.org.
2) *WSJ*, May 31, 2011.
3) *NYT*, November 18, 2011.
4) www.philanthropy.com, November 17, 2011.
5) www.techblog.biz.blogspot.com/2006
6) *WSJ*, August 24, 2011.
7) June 11, 2011.

G. Multipurpose Umbrella Organization

1) Interview with Fraser Nelson in Salt Lake City, February 18, 2012.
2) www.thejerseytomatopress.com, June 28, 2011.

H. Awards to Highlight Values and Inspire Others

3) Darlene M. Siska. "Loud and Clear," *Worth*, May 2007, pp. 76-78.
4) *NYT*, December 11, 2011.
5) *WSJ*, January 27, 2006.
6) *NYT*, June 13, 2011.
7) See www.ncafp.org for other awards and recipients.
8) www.allafrica.com, October 25, 2011.

IV. A. INTERNATIONAL AID TO ENCOURAGE SELF-RELIANCE AND SUSTAINABLE DEVELOPMENT

1) NY, 2011.
2) www.carnegie_council.org, November 21, 2011.

3) *NYT*, November 6, 2011.
4) *NYT*, November 9, 2011.

V. CHOICES AND COMMITMENTS-HOW WILL YOUR CONTRIBUTIONS HAVE THE GREATEST IMPACT?

1) Also consult the Atlantic Philanthropies Report on "Turning Passion into Action: Giving while Living," (www. atlanticphalanthropies.org, June 14, 2010)
2) www.philanthropy.com, August 26, 2011.

Glossary

501 © (3): Internal Revenue Code (IRS) section delineating an organization as charitable and tax-exempt. Among the organizations included are religious, educational, charitable, amateur athletic, scientific or literacy groups, organizations devoted to prevention of cruelty to children or animals. Most organizations searching for foundation or corporate contributions secure a 501 © (3) classification from IRS.

Altruism: The principle or practice of unselfish concern for or devotion to others.

Annual Report: A voluntary report issued by a foundation or corporation that provides data and descriptions for its grant-making activities.

Assets: The amount of capital or principal (money, stocks, bonds, real estate, or other resources) controlled by an individual, foundation or corporate giving program. Usually, the assets are invested, and the resulting income is used for making grants.

Beneficiary: The done or grantee receiving funds from a foundation or other giving programs. This may also refer to society as a whole.

Bequest: A sum of money made available upon the donor's death.

Capital campaign: An organized drive to collect and accumulate substantial funds to finance major needs of a university or other institution or organization, such as a building or a research center.

Challenge grant: A grant made on the condition that other funds will be secured, either on a matching or some other basis, usually within a specific time, in order to stimulate giving from additional donors.

Change Agent: An individual or organization that acts as a catalyst to modify the way things are done.

Charity: Contributions for religion, education, health, alleviating poverty and other causes that benefit the community. Nonprofit organizations for these purposes will be recognized as exempt from federal income tax under Section 501 © (3) of the internal Revenue Code and will be eligible to receive tax-deductible charitable gifts.

Civil Society: The aggregate to non-governmental organizations and institutions that represent the interests and wishes of citizens.

Discretionary Funds: Grant funds distributed at the discretion of one of more officers, trustees, or staff without needing the approval of the full board of directors.

Donee: The recipient of a grant. (Also known as the grantee or the beneficiary.)

Donor: An individual or organization that makes a grant or contribution to a donee. (Also known as the grantor.)

Employee matching grant: A contribution to a charity by an employee that is matched by a similar contribution by his or her employer.

Endowment: Donated funds intended to be in perpetuity to provide income for continued support of a nonprofit organization.

Federated giving program: A joint fundraising effort usually administered by a nonprofit "umbrella" organization that in turn distributes the contributed funds to several nonprofit agencies. United Negro College Fund, and joint arts councils are examples of federated giving programs.

Financial Report: An accounting statement detailing financial data, including income from all sources, expenses, assets and liabilities. Alternatively, an itemized account of how grant funds were used by a donee organization. Most foundations require a financial report from grantees.

Form 990/Form 990-PF: The IRS forms filed annually by public charities and private foundations respectively. The letters PF stand for private foundations. The IRS uses this form to assess compliance with the Internal Revenue Code. Both forms list organization assets, receipts, expenditures, and compensation of officers. Form 990-PF includes a list of grants made during the year by private foundations.

Giving: To transfer or bestow as a gift to another's possession or ownership without compensation. To devote to a cause.

Grant: An award of funds to an organization or individual to undertake charitable activities.

Grassroots fundraising: Efforts to raise money from individuals or groups from the local community on a board basis, usually from people who live in the neighborhood served, through membership drives, auctions, benefits, etc. Donors often feel successful grassroots fundraising means the organization has a lot of community support.

Guidelines: A statement of a foundation's goals, priorities, criteria, and procedures for applying for a grant.

Impact: A continuing, powerful influence to change and improve society through a philanthropic donation and the actual effect it has.

In-Kind Contribution: A donation of goods or services rather than cash or appreciated property.

Letter of Inquiry or Intent: A brief letter outlining an organization's activities and its request for funding that is sent to a prospective donor to determine if it is worth submitting a full grant proposal.

Leverage: Used when a small amount of money is given to attract funding from other sources or to provide the organization with the tools it needs to raise other kinds of funds. Sometimes known as the "multiplier effect."

Microfinance: Providing small loans to low-income people to start and run their own businesses and become financially independent.

Nongovernmental Organization (NGO): A nonprofit organization concerned with improving society that functions outside of government.

Nonprofit Organization: A tax-exempt entity that employs its assets (funds, income, volunteer time, etc.) to promote its goals for improving society.

Philanthropist: A person who contributes money, time, expertise, influence, networks, etc. to nonprofit organizations to promote the common good.

Philanthropy: Comes from the Greek word meaning love of mankind. Mainly refers to voluntary giving by an individual or group to enhance the common good. Contribution are made to nonprofit organizations to found and sustain programs in research, education, combating hunger, promoting arts and culture, and generally improving the quality of life for individuals and the community.

Proposal: A written application, often submitted with supporting documents, requesting a grant from a foundation or other philanthropic entity.

Restricted Funds: Assets or income restricted in its use, in the types of organizations that may receive grants from it, or in the procedures used to make grants from such funds.

Seed Money: a contribution or grant used to launch a new project or organization.

Site Visit: Visiting a donee organization at its office location or area of operation and/or meeting with its staff, directors, or with recipients of its services.

Social Entrepreneur: A businessperson who applies market-based approaches to generate income for social causes without having to rely on philanthropic gifts. Priority is given to innovative ways to bring about social and economic advances.

Spend Down: A philanthropist's or foundation's decision to use up all of the institution and then institution's assets and dissolve it by a certain date.

Strategic Philanthropy: An approach to philanthropy that emphasizes clear goads and instruments for realizing them. It usually includes collecting data to measure impact and sharing the result with others.

Unrestricted Funds: A fund that is not specifically designated for special uses by the donor, or where restrictions have expired or been removed.

Venture Philanthropy: Offering not only funding, but also advice on management, goals, marketing and other strategic ways to succeed. Often connected to social entrepreneurship.

Volunteering: The gift of one's time and efforts without payment.

Major sources consulted for definitions:

Council on Foundations, "Glossary of Philanthropic Terms," *www.cof.org*.
Foundation Center, "Guide to Funding Research." *www.foundationcenter.org/glossary*.
Arrillaga-Andreessen, Laura, Giving 2.0, San Francisco. CA, 2012.

Acknowledgments

I am grateful for the encouragement and helpful advice from Daniel Arnow, Robert A. Belter, Rose Billings, Bonnie Biondi, Philip H. Cohen, Dr. Michael Curtis, Arlene G. Dubin, Dr. Eve Epstein, Susan K. Feagin, Dr. Charlotte K. Frank, Robert Garris, Andrew Gruber, Michael Grzelak, Martin Karlinsky, Donna H. MacPhee, Mark D. Medin, Dr. Anthony W. Marx, Laurens Mendelson, the Hon. Robert M. Morgenthau, Fraser Nelson, Wendy Reilly, Dr. Pola Rosen, Donna Rosenthal, Dr. George D. Schwab, Irving Sitnick, James D. Wolfensohn, Robert S. Yenisey, and Dr. Gary P. Zola.

Other useful comments have come from William Bildner, Sidney Dunn, Kenneth E. Chapin, Dr. Ester Fuchs, Zina Greene, Alina Girshovich, Connie Gruber, Elisa Ho, Harriet Janover, Susan Henshaw Jones, Rick Kaminer, Judith Katz, Ambassador Francis Lorenzo, Dr. David G. Marwell, Ambassador Dr. Josephine Ojiambo, Rabbi Allan Schranz, Dr. George D. Schwab, Fred Schwartz, Paul Sladkus, and Susan Stern,

The CreateSpace teams have contributed immeasurably to the editing, publishing and marketing of the book. They have offered professional expertise and patient coaching at many production stages. Generally, Amazon.com has streamlined the process of bringing treasured ideas to a larger public.

Selected Bibliography

Arrillaga-Andreessen, Laura, *Giving 2.0: Transform Your Giving and our World* (San Francisco, 2012)

Bishop, Matthew & Michael Green, *Philanthrocapitalism: How Giving Can Save the World* (New York, 2008)

Bronfman, Charles & Jeffery Solomon, *The Art of Giving: Where the Soul Meets a Business Plan* (San Francisco, 2010)

Clinton, Bill, *Giving: How Each of Us Can Change the World* (New York, 2007)

Jamal, Azim & Harvey McKinnon, *The Power of Giving: How Giving Back Enriches Us All,* (New York, 2009

Karlan, Dean & Jacob Appel, *How a New Economics is Helping to Solve Global Poverty* (New York, 2011)

Marker, Richard, *Saying "Yes" Wisely: Insights for the Thoughtful Philanthropist* (New York, 2009)

O'Clery, Conor, *The Billionaire Who Wasn't: How Chuck Feeney Secretly Made and Gave Away a Fortune* (New York, 2007)

Sachs, Jeffrey D., *The End of Poverty: Economic Possibilities for our Time* (New York, 2005)

Tierney, Thomas J. and Joel L. Fleishman, *Give Smart: Philanthropy That Gets Results* (New York. 2011)

About the Author

Dr. Susan Aurelia Gitelson has been President of International Consultants. Inc. and has been consulting for international business, educational, cultural and other institutions.

Dr. Gitelson has been Co-Chair of the Dean's Council of the Columbia School of International and Public Affairs (SIPA). She was also a National Vice President of the American Friends of the Hebrew University of Jerusalem and remains a member of the International Board of Governors of the Hebrew University and the Board of the Harry S Truman Research Institute on the Advancement of Peace at the Hebrew University. In addition, she is a member of the Board of Advisers of the National Committee on American Foreign Policy. Currently she is also a member of the Board of Overseers of the Museum of Jewish Heritage/A Living Memorial to the holocaust. Previously she had been on the advisory boards of the Ralph Bunche Institute for International Studies at the City University Graduate Center and the Center for the Study of the Presidency. In addition, she has supported the Columbia SIPA Gitelson Policy Forum, the Gitelson Peace Publications of the Truman Institute, and many other programs and awards at Columbia University, the Hebrew University of Jerusalem, the City University Graduate Center, the Center for the Study of the Presidency and other institutions. Her books and articles have been published on four continents. Columbia University awarded her its prestigious Alumni Medal for Distinguished Service.

Dr. Gitelson received her B.A from Barnard College and her M.I.A. and Ph.D. from Columbia University. She was a trainee at the Rockefeller Foundation. In addition, she was an assistant professor of international relations at the Hebrew University of Jerusalem. Subsequently she headed several small international business firms for many years, where she used her earned income to sponsor cultural and educational programs.

She is the author of *Giving Is Not Just For The Very Rich: A How to Guide for Giving and Philanthropy, and Multilateral Aid Fir National Development And Self-Reliance*. In addition, she co-edited Israel in the Third World with Michael Curtis.

Dr. Gitelson is listed in Who's Who in America, *Who's Who in the World, Who's Who in Finance and Business*, and other biographical directories.

Index

B

C

P

Pam Allyn 20
Pam Omidyar 20, 22, 137
Partnership Project 80, 131
PATHS TO PEACE: Research
  Cooperation Across Borders in the
  Middle East 63
Paul and Daisy M. Soros 58, 137
Paul A. Volcker 85
Paul & Daisy Soros Fellowship for
  New Americans 58, 137
Paul Ichiro Terasaki 68, 137
Paul Jacobs 84, 137
Paul Newman 26, 137
Paul Tudor Jones 18, 137
Peggy Guggenheim 69, 137
Penn State 74, 137
Peter B Lewis 16
Petra Nemcova 21, 137
Pew Environment Group 80, 137
Pew family 84, 137
Philip H. Cohen 6, 122
Philip Johnson 84, 138
Physicians for Social Responsibility
  80, 138
Pierre Omidyar 13, 22, 84, 138
Police Athletic League (PAL) xii
President Bill Clinton 5, 26
President Ellen Johnson Sirleaf of
  Liberia Gbowee 82
Presidential Citizens Medal 36, 138
President John F. Kennedy 28, 138
President Obama 29
president of the Republic of Cape
  Verde, Pedro Verona Pires 85
President Rabbi David Ellenson 46,
  138
President Richard M. Joel 46
President Ronald Reagan 87
Princeton University 16, 138
Priscilla Chan 51
Pritzker Architecture Prize 84, 138
Pritzker family 84, 138

Prof. Benjamin Rivlin 63
Professor David Stark's Center on
  Organizational Innovation (COI)
  62
Professor Hau Lee 93, 138
Professor Jeffrey D. Sachs 91, 138
Professor Louis Henkin 87, 138
Project Appleseed 35, 138
Publicolor 20, 138
Public Service 62, 85, 132, 138
public-society benefit organizations
  4, 76
Pulitzer Prizes 72, 82, 83, 138

Q

Queens College 63, 138

R

Rachel Greene Memorial Fund 53,
  138
Ralph Bunche Institute on the United
  Nations 63, 138
Ramakrishna Mission 46, 138
Ray Chambers 91, 138
Reconstructionist 46, 138
Red Cross 36, 44, 77, 127, 133
Reform 46, 138
Reginald F. Lewis 19, 138
Reginald L. Lewis 19, 138
Renee 65, 138
Richard Barth 50, 138
Richard C. Holbrooke 85, 88
Ricki Tigert Helfer 53, 138
Rita and Gustave Hauser 56
Rita E. Houser 57
Robert A. Belfer 65
Robert E. and Dorothy King 92, 138
Robert K. Weiss 84, 138
Robert M. Morgenthau xii, xiii, 28,
  111, 122, 138
Roberto Perez 37
Robin Hood Foundation 18, 138
Rockefeller Brothers Fund 23, 138